Small Group
Ice-Breakers and
Heart-Warmers

ICE-BREAKERS

— AND —

HEART-WARMERS

By Steve Sheely

101 WAYS TO KICK OFF AND END MEETINGS

SERENDIPITY SMALL GROUP RESOURCES

By

Steve Sheely

SERENDIPITY / Box 1012 / Littleton, CO 80160 / 1-800-525-9563

94 95 96 97 98 / CHG / 5 4 3 2 1

A Quiz

❏ yes ❏ no   Do you feel like your small group does not achieve the level of closeness it should?

❏ yes ❏ no   Do you ever wish for "closure" after you have had a meaningful discussion in a small group?

❏ yes ❏ no   Is it difficult to walk into your home after work and *immediately* begin a heart-to-heart conversation with someone you love about the most important things in your life?

❏ yes ❏ no   Do you think it would be strange to simply walk away from a meaningful conversation right after you have said what you needed to say?

❏ yes ❏ no   Would it feel awkward to sit down in a new small group and immediately answer the question, "How can we pray about our spiritual struggles?"

❏ yes ❏ no   Do you typically take a while to "warm up" before you can talk comfortably about the important issues in your life?

SMALL GROUP CLINIC

❏ yes ❏ no   Does your small group begin "meaty" discussion too abruptly?

❏ yes ❏ no   Does your small group end without a time for prayer requests and prayer?

❏ yes ❏ no   Would a time of affirmation be a positive contribution to your small group experience?

If you answered "yes" to any of these questions this book will be a tremendous help to you and your small group.

Introduction

Small groups are springing up in churches everywhere! Support groups, Bible study groups, 12-step groups, church committees, new member groups...the list goes on and on!

Small groups help people find meaningful relationships in a Christian setting. Small groups can be a supportive community, a family of belonging, and a safe place to grow in Christ.

Creating community in a small group is no accident. With a little planning and some basic principles, a small group can become a healthy place where people can know one another and be known.

This book can help make the small group process happen. By beginning with the right Ice-breaker and ending your meeting with the appropriate closing activity (Heart-Warmer), your small group is well on the way toward becoming a trusting, loving community.

Even if your group is not using material "especially written" for a small group, you can use the Ice-Breakers and Heart-Warmers in this book to make your meeting complete. All you need to do is choose the appropriate Ice-breaker and Heart-warmer for your group!

This book is a collection of Ice-Breakers and Heart-Warmers especially written for a variety of Christian small groups. Some of these activities are Serendipity classics, but many of them are brand new!

Ice-Breakers and Heart-Warmers is a treasure chest full of helpful activities designed to make your small group a place of trust, growth and compassion.

Table of Contents

ICE-BREAKERS

HEART-WARMERS

What Are Ice-Breakers and Heart-Warmers?

Ice-Breakers get the group off to a good start. Instead of jumping immediately into the study and discussion of your group's topic, Ice-Breakers help everyone prepare for the meeting. Ice-Breakers are fun and interesting ways for people to learn more about each other. Ice-Breakers encourage everyone to talk in a lively, non-threatening way. Ice-Breakers help people move out of the business of the day and begin the exciting task of small group conversation.

Imagine your relationships as a house full of rooms. Most day-to-day relationships only visit a few of the rooms. We share information, we talk about the weather, we discuss a purchase, etc. The relationships in a small group can offer much more than that. A healthy small group allows each member to bring more of themselves into the protection of Christian fellowship. A small group should open doors to many rooms, such as playfulness, accountability, prayer, confession, encouragement, affirmation, reminiscing, and dreaming.

An Ice-Breaker begins this process. Ice-Breakers create opportunities for sharing those parts of ourselves we normally keep locked up. Ice-Breakers open doors which remain shut during the day. Ice-Breakers begin an important process: that your small group can be a place where you can let down your guard and be yourself.

During a small group meeting something special should gradually happen. From the time the group gathers to the time they dismiss, a certain magic should occur. Hopefully, by the time the group is ready to close with prayer, the group has become a safe, trusting community. This process, of course, does not happen accidentally.

An Ice-Breaker gets the "community ball" rolling. Bible study and discussion should continue the momentum, moving towards opportunities for personal response to the scripture and the topic. The prayer time should be the culmination of the community building for each meeting. This is a special time, under God's protection, for the group to share their concerns, express gratitude to God, and pray for each other. If the group has moved through the "trust process" during the course of the meeting, the prayer time should be a powerful spiritual experience.

That is why Heart-Warmers are included in this book. If opening a meeting properly is important, ending a meeting is just as important. Heart-Warmers are closing activities which help a group capitalize on their time together.

Heart-Warmers are spiritual. Most people cannot step into a group of people and immediately talk openly about their spiritual lives. Of course, a small group can open with prayer, but it is the prayer at the end of the group which can be the most personal and the most honest.

This book includes dozens of ways a Christian small group can close their meeting in prayer. Affirmation exercises, action plans, and claiming scripture are also powerful closing activities. Each group should choose the Heart-Warmer which is best suited for them.

One book cannot include itineraries for every small group meeting. There are thousands of different types of small groups, each having different forums for study and discussion. However, one book can contain a collection of Ice-Breakers and Heart-Warmers which any small group can use.

Bible study and discussion alone will not necessarily bring a group to a safe place of trust and intimacy. Building a safe, Christian community is a powerful experience, but it is also a delicate process. With an appropriate Ice-Breaker and Heart-Warmer, a small group can be a special place where people can pray, weep, laugh, confess, encourage, and even apply scripture to their lives.

How To Use This Book

Every small group meeting should begin with an Ice-Breaker and end with a Heart-Warmer. While many Ice-Breakers and Heart-Warmers can be used by any group, matching the right exercise to the right group is very helpful as a group matures. Which ones should you select? Here are some of the different traits of your group which will help you choose appropriate Ice-Breakers and Heart-Warmers:

So how do you decide which Ice-Breaker or Heart-Warmer to use for your small group meeting? Actually, choosing the perfect Ice-Breaker or Heart-Warmer is easy. Use the different symbols to help you identify the correct activity for your group. You can find these symbols on the top of each page.

Do you need an Ice-Breaker or a Heart-Warmer?
The first symbol on each page tells you if the exercise is an Ice-Breaker or a Heart-Warmer:

Ice-Breaker

Heart-Warmer

How long has the group been together?
The second symbol on each page tells you if the Ice-Breaker or Heart-Warmer should be used with a new group, an adolescent group, a mature group, or a group that has decided to end.

New Group

3 Months to 1 Year

Mature Group

Group that has decided to end

Generally speaking, Ice-Breakers and Heart-Warmers for new groups will seek less disclosure and risk than more mature groups. Groups that have decided to end also need special help to close their group properly.

What type of group is it?

Sometimes the type of your small group can help you determine the type of Ice-Breaker or Heart-Warmer you should choose. An Ice-Breaker or Heart-Warmer which uses these symbols will work well with the particular type of group.

New Member Group

Discipleship Group

Support Groups

What is the topic of your meeting?

Matching the topic of the Ice-Breaker and Heart-Warmer with the topic of the current discussion can make the small group meeting more meaningful for everyone. Look for the following symbols which identify the topic of the Ice-Breakers and Heart-Warmers. Some Ice-Breakers and Heart-Warmers will have more than one of these symbols:

Stress and Time

Relationships

General Information

Memories

Families

Christian Basics

Money and Success

Emotions

Self-awareness

Heart-Warmers might have some different topics, such as:

Accountability

Self-Affirmation

Prayer Styles

Bible Promises

Affirming Others

Group Appreciation

What is the mood of your group?
Sometimes your group needs a certain type of Ice-Breaker or Heart-Warmer to match its particular mood. These symbols will help you find the perfect exercise:

Fun

Serious

Sharing Questions

Sometimes an Ice-Breaker or Heart-Warmer will have more than one symbol from each category. This tells you that it can be used in more than one way.

Helpful Hints

Here are some hints which will help you make the most out of this book:

1. Each group member should feel free to elaborate on his or her responses to the Ice-Breakers and Heart-Warmers.

2. The leader might begin the Ice-Breaker or Heart-Warmer time with instructions about time, such as "We have enough time for each person to talk about their answers for 3 minutes."

3. Feel free to "pass" at any time if you do not want to talk.

4. You might need to adapt or change an Ice-Breaker or Heart-Warmer to fit the specific needs of your group. Be creative!

5. Feel free to use the same Ice-Breaker or Heart-Warmer more than once.

6. Doing an Ice-Breaker at the beginning and the end of the meeting is a possibility. This can reveal how people's feelings can change over the course of a small group meeting.

7. You might wish to use several Ice-Breakers or Heart-Warmers for an entire meeting!

8. Certain Ice-Breakers and Heart-Warmers could be connected, using a particular Ice-Breaker with a matching Heart-Warmer.

9. Look for the "♥" at the bottom of the page of some Ice-Breakers. The heart indicates special suggestions to make a Heart-Warmer out of that Ice-Breaker. For example, if the Ice-Breaker is about time management, the "♥" might tell you to end your meeting by praying about all the different tasks in your life.

10. Use extra care when using Ice-Breakers and Heart-Warmers in certain support groups, recovery groups, shame-based groups, or other sensitive issue groups. Some of the Ice-Breakers and Heart-Warmers ask questions about families, relationships, past experiences, etc. which might be difficult for some people to answer freely.

11. Use a variety of Ice-Breakers and Heart-Warmers. This will help people express different feelings, memories, dreams and ideas.

12. Sometimes the group leader will need to be the "guinea pig." This means that the group leader should be the first one to try a particular Ice-Breaker or Heart-Warmer.

Tips for a Successful Small Group

Use this checklist to see if your small group is on the right track:

❑ Are you using Ice-Breakers which fit your group at each meeting ?

❑ Are you using Heart-Warmers which are carefully chosen for your group at the end of each meeting ?

❑ Are you using these principles of Bible study...

   • Do your discussion questions gradually allow for more and more personal disclosure?

   • Do your discussion questions require only "right or wrong" answers? Or are they open questions which give people the freedom to answer from their personal experience?

   • Do your discussions questions ever allow multiple choice options so everyone, no matter how much they know the Bible, can answer without being embarrassed?

   • Do you ever divide into foursomes so your group members can talk openly without being intimidated by talking in front of the entire group?

❑ Do you have a balanced group, which includes Bible study, group-building, and mission?

❑ Are you using a group covenant like the one on the next page?

❑ Do your group members avoid unsolicited judging, advice-giving, and problem solving?

Group Covenant

A group covenant is a valuable tool for any small group. The group covenant can help make sure that every group member has the same idea about what the group is all about. It keeps all the group members "on the same page."

When a group has their first meeting, or after a previous covenant has expired, the group should spend some time answering the following questions. The group covenant involves a process which includes everyone in decision-making. If everyone joins in the discussion and has input in the group covenant, no one will feel left out and everyone will feel like they have had a part in the direction the group is taking.

The purpose of our group is...

The goals of our group are...

We will meet for _____ weeks, after which we will decide if we wish to continue as a group. If we do decide to continue, we will reconsider this covenant.

We will meet _____ (weekly, bi-monthly, monthly).

Our meetings will begin at _____ o'clock and we will strive to start and end on time.

We will meet at _____ or rotate house-to-house.

We will take care of the following details:

❑ Childcare ❑ Refreshments ❑ Group Material

We will agree to the following rules for our small group:

❑ **Priority**: While we are in this group we will give group meetings priority.

❑ **Participation**: Everyone is given the right to their own opinion and "dumb questions" are respected.

❑ **Confidentiality**: Anything said in the meeting is never to be repeated outside the meeting.

❑ **Empty Chair**: The group stays open to new people as long as group size and space requirements allow.

❑ **Support**: Permission is given to call each other in times of need.

❑ **Ministry Project**: We agree to choose and complete a ministry project.

I Am Somebody Who...

Look over this list and mark five things which describe you. When everyone is finished, put your booklet in a stack in the middle of the group. After the booklets are piled up, take turns taking a booklet from the pile. Go around the group and take turns reading the five things marked in your booklet and see if the group can guess who the booklet belongs to.

I am somebody who...

- ❏ blushes at a compliment
- ❏ would go on a blind date
- ❏ enjoys a professional massage
- ❏ sings in the shower
- ❏ will tell someone their fly is open
- ❏ slurps my soup
- ❏ listens to music full blast
- ❏ likes to dance
- ❏ cries at movies
- ❏ stops to smell the flowers
- ❏ daydreams a lot
- ❏ avoids discussions about sex
- ❏ has placed a personal ad
- ❏ likes kissing on the first date
- ❏ won't use a public toilet
- ❏ likes thunderstorms
- ❏ enjoys romance novels
- ❏ loves crossword puzzles
- ❏ falls in love quickly
- ❏ hates flying
- ❏ would enjoy skydiving
- ❏ has a black belt
- ❏ watches soap operas
- ❏ is afraid of the dark
- ❏ goes to bed early
- ❏ will ask a stranger for directions
- ❏ would tell a friend they have bad breath

- ❏ talks to plants
- ❏ sleeps until the last second
- ❏ ask a stranger for directions
- ❏ likes to travel alone
- ❏ reads the financial page
- ❏ saves for a rainy day
- ❏ lies about my age
- ❏ yells at the umpire
- ❏ fixes my own car
- ❏ would marry someone of another race
- ❏ closes my eyes at horror movies
- ❏ thumps cantaloupes
- ❏ worries constantly about my kids
- ❏ makes a "to do" list each morning
- ❏ cheats at monopoly
- ❏ would vacation at home
- ❏ has a pen pal
- ❏ sleeps with a teddy bear
- ❏ would prefer to be cremated
- ❏ has never had an operation
- ❏ tells a friend they have bad breath
- ❏ likes to play practical jokes
- ❏ will wear curlers to the store
- ❏ reads the comics before the front page
- ❏ is always sending greeting cards
- ❏ eats dessert first

My Roles

Everyone has many roles in their life. Help your group get to know you better by telling them all the roles in your life.

I am a...

❑ Father	❑ Boss	❑ Hobbyist
❑ Mother	❑ Landlord	❑ Homeowner
❑ Brother	❑ Tenant	❑ Auto Operator
❑ Sister	❑ Political Activist	❑ Small Group member
❑ Husband	❑ Taxpayer	❑ Worker
❑ Wife	❑ Church member	❑ Step-parent
❑ Friend	❑ Club member	❑ Step-child
❑ Pet Owner	❑ Student	❑ In-law
❑ Employee	❑ Volunteer	❑ Other: _____

Which of these roles in the most fun?

The most challenging?

The most rewarding?

The most frustrating?

Well, Let Me Tell You About My Day. . .

What was your day like today? Or your week? Month? Year? Use one of the items below to help you describe your day to the group. Feel free to elaborate. . .

Greek Tragedy

Episode of 3 Stooges

Soap Opera

Clint Eastwood Movie

Bible Epic

Late Night News

Fireworks Display

Professional Wrestling Match

Boring Lecture

Fairy Tale

KWIZ

Choose one of the following subjects and mark your answers for each question. Then your group will take turns trying to guess each others answers. For each correct answer, the guesser receives the dollar amount for that question. After everyone is finished, add up your winnings and see who has the most money.

HEALTH

For $1, I can best be described as a. . .
❑ Health nut
❑ Junk food junkie

For $2, I am more likely to. . .
❑ Jog
❑ Swim
❑ Do aerobics

For $3, my favorite part about exercise is. . .
❑ Wearing spandex
❑ Meeting people at the gym
❑ Improving my stamina
❑ Scolding people who do not workout

For $4, no matter how healthy it is, I will never eat. . .
❑ Bean sprouts   ❑ Tofu
❑ Wheat germ   ❑ Liver
❑ Yogurt   ❑ Granola

SLEEP HABITS

For $1, I dream. . .
❑ In color
❑ In black and white

For $2, I. . .
❑ Snore
❑ Don't snore
❑ Don't know

For $3, I am more likely to use. . .
❑ A small pillow
❑ A large pillow
❑ No pillow
❑ A bunch of pillows

For $4, in order to get to sleep, I. . .
❑ Count sheep   ❑ Watch TV
❑ Read a book   ❑ Play solitaire
❑ Do crossword puzzles
❑ Wait until I'm exhausted

MONEY

For $1, I can best be described as. . .
❑ A spender
❑ A saver

For $2, I would rather carry. . .
❑ A big wad of small bills
❑ No cash at all
❑ A few large bills

For $3, When I have extra change. . .
❑ I spend it
❑ I save it for a rainy day
❑ I lose it
❑ I look for rare coins

For $4, If I won a million dollars, I. . .
❑ Wouldn't tell anyone
❑ Would tell everyone I was a millionaire
❑ Would buy more lottery tickets
❑ Would not change my lifestyle
❑ Would move
❑ Would buy a house

more on next page

SOCIAL EVENTS

For $1, when I get an invitation with "R.S.V.P.," I . . .
❑ Usually call
❑ Forget to call

For $2, I prefer attending. . .
❑ A black tie gala
❑ Casual Cook-out
❑ Cocktail party

For $3, I most enjoy events. . .
❑ With 1 or 2 close friends
❑ Several good friends
❑ A bunch of friends and acquaintances
❑ Hundreds of perfect strangers

For $4, at a social gathering, I would rather. . .
❑ Mingle
❑ Sing along around the piano
❑ Go on a scavenger hunt
❑ Eat dinner
❑ make new friends
❑ Talk about the weather

BIRTHDAYS

For $1, for my birthday, I would rather get. . .
❑ No presents
❑ Lots of presents

For $2, I would prefer. . .
❑ A big, planned party
❑ Surprise party
❑ No party

For $3, my favorite type of birthday cake is. . .
❑ Chocolate cake with chocolate icing
❑ Angel food cake
❑ Carrot cake with cream cheese icing
❑ Yellow cake with white frosting

For $4, The game I would rather play at my birthday is. . .
❑ Pin the tail on the donkey
❑ Spin the bottle
❑ Twister
❑ Charades
❑ Pictionary
❑ Croquet

TV SHOWS

For $1, I am more likely to. . .
❑ Hog the remote
❑ Share the remote

For $2, my viewing habits can best be described as. . .
❑ Couch potato
❑ Channel surfer
❑ Highly selective

For $3, I am most likely to watch. . .
❑ A glitzy game show
❑ A sassy sitcom
❑ A wild western
❑ A noteworthy news show

For $4, my favorite TV show is. . .
❑ Meet the Press
❑ As the World Turns
❑ Beverly Hills 90210
❑ Bugs Bunny cartoon
❑ Gilligan's Island
❑ Roseanne

more on next page

EATING HABITS

For $1, at a formal meal I. . .
- ❏ Know which fork to use
- ❏ Don't know where to put my napkin

For $3, I would rather eat. . .
- ❏ 1 big meal & 2 light meals
- ❏ 3 similar sized meals
- ❏ 2 large meals & 1 small meal
- ❏ several light meals & snacks

For $2, I. . .
- ❏ Eat fast
- ❏ Eat slow
- ❏ Eat dessert first

For $4, I get grossed out when people. . .
- ❏ Slurp their soup
- ❏ Cough at the table
- ❏ Smack their lips
- ❏ Talk with mouth full
- ❏ Have food on their teeth
- ❏ Leave lipstick on their glass

READING NEWSPAPER

For $1, I am more likely to. . .
- ❏ just scan the headlines
- ❏ read the entire story

For $3, my favorite part of the paper is. . .
- ❏ the sports section
- ❏ Ann Landers
- ❏ the financial section
- ❏ the crossword puzzle

For $2, when I finish reading the paper, I usually. . .
- ❏ leave it on the floor
- ❏ throw it away
- ❏ recycle

For $4, my favorite comic strip is. . .
- ❏ Garfield
- ❏ Blondie
- ❏ Prince Valiant
- ❏ Cathy
- ❏ Calvin and Hobbes
- ❏ Peanuts

HOLIDAYS

For $1, I am more inspired by. . .
- ❏ Christmas
- ❏ Easter

For $3, I would rather spend a holiday. . .
- ❏ By myself taking it easy
- ❏ With my family having a big dinner
- ❏ With a bunch of friends at a picnic
- ❏ At a huge public event like a parade

For $2, I enjoy holidays that are. . .
- ❏ Sentimental
- ❏ Inspirational
- ❏ Patriotic

For $4, my favorite holiday from this list is. . .
- ❏ Martin Luther King Jr. Day
- ❏ Columbus Day
- ❏ Arbor Day
- ❏ Labor Day
- ❏ Memorial Day
- ❏ National Pickle Day

The Jitters

Joining a new small group can be a difficult experience. Your group might want to talk about some of these feelings. Answer the questions listed below and then go around the group and share some of your answers. This might be a good Ice-Breaker to use when your group is preparing to work on the group covenant.

When I enter a room full of people I don't know very well I usually feel ...

When I am feeling anxious in a new situation I usually ...

I am here because ...

I would feel more comfortable with a leader who ...

The things that concern me most about joining groups are ...

When I'm nervous I feel ...

Rules make me feel ...

I am more likely to get involved in a group when ...

Right now I'm feeling ...

Osmosis

Pair up with another group member and sit back-to-back with your chairs facing opposite directions. Take turns answering the four questions below:

What is your middle name and how did you get it?

Where did you live when you were ten years old and what was your favorite thing to do in the summer?

What is the best job you've ever had?

What is your favorite possession?

After you have both answered these four questions, return to your group. Spend a moment guessing how your partner might answer these questions:

If _____ had a day off, he/she is likely to spend the day. . .

If _____'s house was on fire, one thing he/she is certain to rescue is. . .

When _____ goes to the circus, his/her favorite part is. . .

If _____ could live anywhere in the world, it would be. . .

Take turns sharing your guesses with the group and then let your partner tell everyone how accurate you were.

How'd It Go Today?

What kind of day did you have today? Mark where you fit on each of the lines below which best describes the kind of day you've had today. Then go around the group and explain why you marked what you did.

Barefoot in the Park _ _ _ _ _ _ _ _ _ _ _ _ _ _Nightmare on Elm Street

Sunny _Stormy

I felt like a princess _ _ _ _ _ _ _ _ _ _ _ _ _ _ _ _ _I felt like a gym shoe

Miss America _Bad hair day

Ants _Grasshopper

Wonder Dog _Fire Hydrant

Baseball _Louisville Slugger

Tasmanian Devil _Rip Van Winkle

King Midas _Court Jester

Mother Theresa _Madonna

Statue _Pigeon

Human Bingo

After the leader says "Go!" ask people in the group if they have ever done or can do the following things. If someone answers "yes" to this question, have them sign their initials in that box. Continue until someone completes a row, column or diagonal and yells "BINGO." Then keep playing for a total of 10 minutes and see who has the most boxes.

can juggle	TP'd a house	ever used an outhouse	sing in the shower	rec'd 6+ traffic tickets	ever paddled in school	watched Sesame Street
ever slept in church	ever changed a diaper	split pants in public	milked a cow	born out of the country	have been to Hawaii	can do the splits
watches soap operas	can touch tongue to nose	driven a motor-cycle	never ridden a horse	moved twice last year	sleeps on a waterbed	now has hole in sock
walked in wrong restroom	loves classical music	ever skipped school	FREE	ever broke a leg	have a hot tub	love eating sushi
is an only child	loves junk food	has a 3- inch + scar	wears P.J.'s	ever smoked a cigar	been skinny- dipping	weighs under 110
likes writing poetry	still has tonsils	can quote a Bible verse	likes bubble baths	wearing Fruit of the Loom	doesn't use mouth wash	often watches cartoons
doesn't like kissing	can wiggle ears	can play the guitar	plays chess regularly	only reads the comics	can touch palms to floor	sleeps w/ stuffed animals

The Grand Total

This is a fun Ice-Breaker that has additional uses. You can use this Ice-Breaker to divide your group into two subgroups (odds and evens). You can also calculate who has the highest and lowest totals if you need a fun way to select someone to do a particular task, such as bring refreshments or be first to tell their story.

Fill each box with the correct number and then total your score. When everyone is finished, go around the group and explain how you got your total.

☐ +		☐ +	
Number of wrecks you have been in		Number of pictures on your refrigerator	
☐ -		☐ +	
Number of pets you own		Number of weddings you've been in	
☐ +		☐ -	
Number of times you were sent to the principal's office as a child		Number of photo albums you own	
☐ +		☐ -	
Number of animal sounds you can make		Number of brothers and sisters you have (including stepbrothers and stepsisters)	
☐ +		☐ -	
Number of volunteer organizations you have helped		Date of the month you were born on	
☐ =		☐	
Number of balls you can juggle		Grand Total	

The 4 Quaker Questions

This is an old Quaker activity which Serendipity has adapted over the years. Go around the group and share your answers to the questions, one at a time. This Ice - Breaker has been known to take between 30 and 60 minutes for some groups.

Where were you living between the ages of seven and twelve and what were the winters like then?

How was your home heated during that time?

What was the center of warmth in your life when you were a child? (It could be a place in the house, a time of year, a person, etc.)

When did God become a "warm" person to you. . . and how did it happen?

Brain Food

Congratulations! You have won a gift certificate for a free class at a local junior college. You get to take any course they offer! What would you choose? What would be your last choice? Why? Before you share your choice with your group, let them guess what course you would choose. . .

Archaeology 714: "Bones Down Under: The study of aboriginal fossils in Australia." Dr. Foster. Prerequisite: Archaeology 602, "Providing Data For Your Professor's Latest Book." Shovels provided.

Bird-Watching 101: "Birds Are Our Friends." In this introduction you will learn what a bird looks like, how many wings it has and how to identify a feather. BYOB (binoculars). Prerequisites: none. Tests: none. Term papers: none. Professor: none.

Political Science 403: "The Management of a Bureaucracy." An introduction to bureaucratic language, form-making and standing in line. Special segments will include "How to get a driver's license" and "You can't fight city hall until you can find a parking place." Ann R. Kay. Prerequisites: Surviving enrollment or equivalent.

Calculus 555: "The Mathematics of Chaos." This class meets in several different locations at several different times and is taught by several different professors. Prerequisites: Literature 101, Ceramics and gym. Dr. Seuss.

Creative Writing 102: "The Limerick." There once was a student in school, Who thought he was totally cool. Then he took this class, and he did not pass. Now everyone thinks he's a fool. Prerequisite: Creative Writing 121, "The Food Label."

Sociology 313: "T.V. Viewing in America." A fascinating sociological study of television viewing at its finest. Special sections will focus on becoming the quintessential couch potato, snacking and viewing habits, and channel surfing. The art of classifying and reciting selections from classic reruns will also be addressed.

Applied Behavioral Sciences 101: "Remedial Self-Improvement." This course will introduce the student in the language of psychobabble and beginning navel-gazing skills. Students will be encouraged to realize how miserable they are and how much they need expensive therapy. Dr. Ziggy.

Radio, Television & Film 202: "Movie Snacks." This class is a serious investigation of popcorn, goo-goo clusters, Whoppers, and Good'n Fruity in the 20th Century American film experience. Prerequisite: Radio, Television & Film 132, "Finding a Seat at the Theatre." Dr. Hitchcock.

Car Repair 104: "Automotive Electronics." This course is for serious students only. The first part of the semester will be devoted to setting the buttons on your car radio. The second part of the course will focus on how to use intermittent wipers. Prerequisite: Home Repair 499, "Setting the Clock on your VCR" or equivalent. Dr. Goodwrench.

My Relationships

How are you doing in your relationships? Choose a "circle" of relationships, such as family, co-workers, friends, small group members, etc. Among the pictures below, select the ones which best describe your recent behavior among the relationships you have chosen. Tell the group how you see yourself in those relationships. Tell the group how the other people in the relationships you have chosen might see you.

St. Nick
All I do is give, give, give

Teddy Bear
I seem to comfort people

Grinch
I seem to ruin
everyone's fun

Benedict Arnold
I feel like a traitor

Selfish Shellfish
Keep your hands off my pearl!

Aladdin's Genie
I can grant wishes!

Mickey Mouse
I listen so much I'm all ears!

A Doormat
People have been
wiping their feet on me

Grizzly Bear
Watch out! I may bite!

Mother Hen
Cluck! Who needs me now?

Saint Sweetheart
I couldn't be nicer

Feelings and Faces

How do you feel? How did you feel when you walked into your small group meeting? How do you feel after it is over? Choose a face that describes how you feel, or draw a face that shows how you are feeling. Tell your group why you chose the face that you did.

happy

anxious

frustrated

excited

thrilled

in love

jolly

ambivalent

peaceful

sad

angry

great

stressed

lonely

unsure

lousy

pensive

cautious

Hidden Talent

Everyone has a talent. What is your secret talent? What talents do you have that you can show the group? Can you wiggle your ears, raise one eyebrow, stand on your head, or touch your nose with your tongue?

Son of KWIZ

Choose one of the following subjects and mark your answers for each question. Then your group will take turns trying to guess each other's answers. For each correct answer, the guesser will receive the dollar amount for that question. After everyone is finished, add up your winnings and see who has the most money.

PETS

For $1, in my opinion, the cutest animal is. . .
❑ A puppy
❑ A kitten

For $2, if I could choose a dog, I would select. . .
❑ A frisky, little dog
❑ A big, playful dog
❑ A purebred dog

For $3, what bugs me about having a pet is. . .
❑ Cleaning up the mess
❑ When they are noisy
❑ Finding hair or feathers everywhere
❑ When they scratch things

For $4, my favorite type of pet is a. . .
❑ A snake   ❑ A parrot
❑ A pot-bellied pig   ❑ Gerbils
❑ A lizard   ❑ A monkey

DRIVING/TRAFFIC

For $1, I could best be described as. . .
❑ Cautious Casey
❑ Racy Randy

For $2, I am probably more likely to. . .
❑ Speed
❑ Roll through a stop sign
❑ Zoom through a yellow light

For $3, the last time I got a speeding ticket was. . .
❑ Within the last month
❑ Never
❑ Within the last six months
❑ Over a year ago

For $4, my pet peeve when it comes to driving is. . .
❑ People who don't use a turn signal
❑ Rush hour traffic
❑ Speeders in residential neighborhoods
❑ Slow traffic in the left lane
❑ Sunday drivers
❑ People who drive while talking on their car phones

More on next page

SHOPPING

For $1, I am more likely to. . .
❑ Buy, Buy, Buy!
❑ Browse

For $2, I would rather shop at. . .
❑ Fancy boutiques
❑ The mall
❑ Huge discount stores

For $3, I would rather buy. . .
❑ 1 very fancy item
❑ 2 nice things
❑ Several inexpensive things
❑ A whole lot of cheap stuff

For $4, my favorite type of store is a. . .
❑ Shoe store   ❑ Furniture store
❑ Bookstore   ❑ Hardware store
❑ Music store   ❑ Clothes store

SPORTING EVENTS

For $1, I would prefer. . .
❑ To watch a Big League event
❑ To play a backyard game

For $2, at a live sporting event, I am more likely to. . .
❑ Yell at the ref
❑ Paint my face and dance around
❑ Do the wave

For $3, my favorite ball park food is. . .
❑ Hot dogs
❑ Nachos
❑ Popcorn
❑ Pretzels

For $4, one sport I would never try is. . .
❑ Bungee jumping   ❑ Rugby
❑ Ski jumping   ❑ Sky diving
❑ Scuba diving
❑ Professional wrestling

READING

For $1, I would rather read. . .
❑ A novel I can't put down
❑ A book full of valuable facts

For $2, my favorite type of non-fiction book is. . .
❑ A biography
❑ A travelogue
❑ History

For $3, when I put a book away that I'm still reading I. . .
❑ Fold the corner of the page
❑ Lay the book down on the open page
❑ Use a book mark
❑ Write the page number down

For $4, my favorite type of fiction book is. . .
❑ A mystery novel
❑ Science fiction
❑ Scary thrillers
❑ A romance novel
❑ Action/adventure
❑ Anything with pictures

More on next page

OUTDOORS

For $1, I would rather go see the. . .
❑ Mountains
❑ Beach

For $2, I would rather stay in a . . .
❑ Tent
❑ Motorhome
❑ Cabin

For $3, when I go camping I prefer to. . .
❑ Go hiking
❑ Take photographs
❑ Go swimming
❑ Do nothing

For $4, my favorite food when I spend time outdoors is. . .
❑ S'mores
❑ Oatmeal
❑ Granola with M&Ms
❑ Hot, spicy chili
❑ Freeze-dried spaghetti
❑ Wieners cooked over a campfire

COLORS

For $1, I prefer. . .
❑ Bright, bold colors
❑ Soft pastel colors

For $2, I am more drawn to. . .
❑ Polka dots
❑ Plaids
❑ Stripes

For $3, the colorful thing I enjoy the most is. . .
❑ A rainbow
❑ A sunset
❑ A bouquet of flowers
❑ A fireworks display

For $4, my favorite color is. . .
❑ Red   ❑ Blue
❑ Orange   ❑ Purple
❑ Green   ❑ Yellow
❑ Pink   ❑ Other

GAMES

For $1, I prefer. . .
❑ Exciting, action games
❑ Clever, board games

For $2, my favorite indoor game is. . .
❑ Checkers   ❑ Monopoly
❑ Scrabble   ❑ Dominoes

For $3, the outdoor game I would rather play is. . .
❑ Croquet
❑ Frisbee
❑ Volleyball
❑ Hide and seek

For $4, the game I would not like to play is. . .
❑ Truth or dare
❑ Twister
❑ Charades
❑ Spin the bottle
❑ Egg toss
❑ Dog pile

Dream Job

What would you do if you could choose any career? Look at the list below and choose a career you would rather do. What was your dream career when you were 10 years old? Feel free to choose a career that is not listed. After you have chosen your dream job, let other group members take turns guessing what you have selected.

Police Officer
A brave upholder of the law
in an exciting fight against criminals.

Astronaut
A daring outer-space pilot
and extra-terrestrial scientist.

Actor/Actress
A glamorous movie star who gets big
money to appear on the silver screen.

Minister
A beloved servant who takes care
of a congregation's spiritual needs.

High-Powered Attorney
An eloquent, intelligent spokesperson
of the law who defends the
innocent in the courtroom

Race Car Driver
A handsome, courageous competitor
who tears around the track at
200 m.p.h.

Politician
A high-profile public servant who can
whip out a clever deal or an
inspiring speech at the drop of a hat.

Veterinarian
The beloved animal doctor
everyone trusts with
their pets and livestock

Fashion Model
A jet-setting career for those with a
striking presence and an alluring smile.

Novelist
The fiction writer who can produce
bestsellers that everyone talks about.

TV Evangelist
An expert preacher and fundraiser
who is the pastor of the airwaves.

Social Worker
The steward of government resources
who strives to help the unfortunate
get back on their feet

Banker
The respected lender who can
help someone fulfill their
greatest dreams.

Doctor
The family physician who is a trusted
healer, devoted listener and
close friend.

Missionary
The bold preacher who is willing
to go around the world to
share the gospel.

Jet Pilot
Streaking across the sky in a
screaming jet, ready to
defend the nation.

Psychologist
The trusted counselor who helps
people come to peace with
themselves.

Developer
A visionary who can see a
building, a resort, or
subdivision where one does not exist.

Teacher
The educator who inspires their
students to expand their horizons
and see the world.

Computer Jockey
To boldly write software
programs that no one has
has written before.

My Ideal Room

If you could design an ideal room for yourself, what kind of room would it be? If you could custom design this room, what would it look like?

After everyone imagines their ideal room, let the group guess the type of room you would choose before you describe your ideal room.

Ballroom. A grand hall with parquet floors, chandeliers and beautiful velvet curtains. Perfect for hosting the most elegant events.

Greenhouse. A glass-walled jungle with built-in sprinklers and full of lush, exotic tropical plants and flowers.

Dining room. The perfect room for entertaining your guests with a wonderful meal. A long mahogany table surrounded by hand-carved highback chairs highlights this room.

Studio. With plenty of windows and skylights, this airy studio is full of natural light. You'll find plenty of room for painting, sculpting, dancing or any of your creative pursuits.

Workshop. Imagine a room full of all the tools you'll ever need, neatly arranged in this spacious shop. You could make anything in here!

Playroom. This brightly colored room is full of toys, games, stuffed animals and bean bag chairs. Invite all your friends over for a great time in this room full of fun!

Bedroom. It's the ultimate bedroom, complete with huge walk-in closets. You'll find a king-sized bed, nightstands full of books, and plenty of convenient switches and remote controls.

Living room. This elegant room includes luxurious sofas, a china cabinet, coffee tables, ornamental rugs, paintings and vases. This is the perfect room for chatting with your guests and drinking coffee.

Bathroom. It's like your own spa, complete with glass bricks, ceramic tile, jacuzzi, and a dry sauna. You'll also find soft, comfy towels, aromatic soaps and sumptuous lotions.

Home Theatre. Have a seat in front of your high-definition, big-screen TV with Dolby Surround Sound. You can listen to your favorite movies, CDs or FM stereo through your hi-fidelity speakers.

Study. It's the ultimate home library and the ultimate home office. You'll find all your favorite books, a high-powered personal computer and a fax machine. Not to mention a comfy chair for reading!

Kitchen. The gourmet's delight! Restaurant quality stove and refrigerator, copper pots and pans and plenty of counter space. You'll also find huge pantries to hold all your cooking materials.

A Bunch'a Bests

This is your very own Awards Show! You get to give awards to all the great people and great things from your life! Think of the "bests" in your life and write them down. Choose 2 or 3 of them and tell the group why these things are special to you.

The best friend I had as a kid. . .

The best teacher I ever had. . .

The best job I ever had. . .

The best boss I ever had. . .

The best toy I ever had. . .

The best class I ever took in school. . .

The best book I ever read or movie I ever saw. . .

The best pet I've ever had. . .

The best birthday I ever had. . .

The best car I ever had. . .

The best vacation I've ever taken. . .

The best neighbor I've ever had. . .

I'm Just a Kid!

You are 11 years old. Who are you? What do you like to do? If the group could meet you as an 11-year-old kid, what would you be like? Answer the following situations and tell the group your answers:

It's your 11th birthday! Yum, a birthday cake! What kind is it? You blow out the candles easily. What did you wish for? What is your "dream" present?

Your father or guardian is returning from a day of work. What does he do? What do you want to be when you grow up?

Yahoo! The teachers are at a convention today! What are you going to do? Who do you want to do it with?

It's Friday. Your best friend is coming over to spend the night! What is his/her name? What is he/she like? What do you like most about this friend?

Summer is here! Where is your family going on vacation? Are you getting there by car? What's it like in the car? Where are you going? What is your favorite thing about this place?

The recess bell has rung! What are you going to do?

Think of a kindly older person on your street. How would they describe you when you were 11?

How's the Weather?

Consider the different areas of your life. Assign a month of the year to each one. Tell the group what month it is in several areas of your life. Feel free to explain why you chose what you did.

Romance	Career	Relational
Financial	Spiritual	Family Life
Emotional	Intellectual	Overall

January: cold and snowy, but a new year is on the way.

February: The bleakest time of the year. The color gray is getting old.

March: Cold and blustery, but there is a sniff of spring in the air.

April: Tumultuous and stormy, but life is breaking out everywhere.

May: Spring has sprung! The flowers are blooming and the skies are full of sunlight and cool breezes.

June: It's pleasantly warm, things are growing and people are beginning to take vacations.

July: Boy, it's hot. Everything is smoldering and oppressive.

August: The heat has settled in. We sure could use some rain.

September: The first cool breezes of fall can be felt, but it sure is warm. There is change in the air.

October: Autumn has arrived. Life is beginning to hibernate, but the colors are still beautiful.

November: The leaves have fallen and it's getting cold.

December: Even though it's cold and desolate-looking outside, the holidays keep things festive.

Inspiration

Pair up with a member of your group and answer the following questions. When you are finished, return to your group and take turns telling the group how your partner answered the questions.

I get inspired by. . .

Being Outdoors

Triumphant Music

Reading the Bible

Brainstorming With Others

Being Artistic

Reading an Uplifting Book

Worship Service

Gorgeous Sunset

Taking a Walk

Praying

One especially profound moment of inspiration in my life was when. . .

Right now, I could be inspired by. . .

This group is inspiring to me because. . .

Twenty (Sharing) Questions (Part 1)

Sometimes all a group needs to get rolling is a sharing question. Sharing questions are read to the group and then each group member spends a few moments answering. After your group has answered a question, check the box so you can remember if that question has been discussed.

❑ 1. What is your favorite food? What is your least favorite food? What is the favorite meal you've ever had?

❑ 2. What was the high point of your week? What was the low point?

❑ 3. What is your favorite place in the house and why?

❑ 4. What is one job you enjoy doing around the house?

❑ 5. What hobby did you enjoy in your teens?

❑ 6. What is your middle name? Where did you get it?

❑ 7. What was your first job?

❑ 8. What is the worst storm or disaster you have ever been in?

❑ 9. What is the funniest thing that ever happened in a religious setting?

❑ 10. What's your favorite thing to do on a rainy day?

❑ 11. What is your most prized possession? Why?

❑ 12. What is the best costume you've worn to a costume party?

❑ 13. What was the most disastrous meal that you've ever eaten or made?

❑ 14. Describe your first blind date. What happened?

❑ 15. What was your worst home-decorating/fix-it experience?

❑ 16. Who was your weirdest neighbor? Why?

❑ 17. What was your home town like?

❑ 18. If you were an animal, which one would you like to be? Why?

❑ 19. What was your favorite teen hangout?

❑ 20. What was your first car like?

My Museum

Congratulations! A wealthy committee of good-hearted citizens has decided to build a museum in your honor! The museum has been built and now it is up to you to help create the displays.

The museum has several different exhibits:

Family Heritage
Childhood
High School
Romance
Accomplishments
Spiritual Life
The Future (under construction)

Think of one memento from your life that will be in each exhibit of your museum. For the exhibit called, "The Future," what do you hope to show some day? Take turns going around the group and telling everyone what is on display in your personal museum and why.

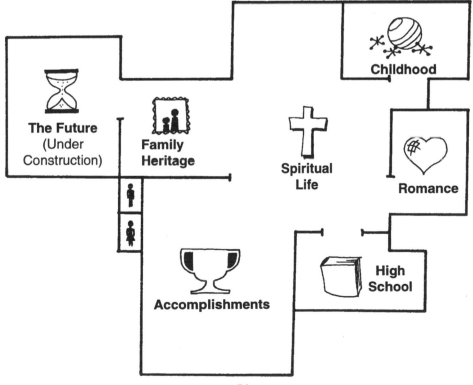

What Would You Do?

Choose one of the following fantasy situations. After you have read the situation, imagine how you would complete the story. Jot down a few notes about what you would do in that situation.

Go around the group and tell which situation you have chosen. Let one or two group members guess how you might complete that situation, then explain what you would do.

Wild, Wild West

You are a rancher with 500 head of cattle in the Montana hills. You go to town one day with your sidekick Mel to buy some feed. Mel wanders off and you find him flirting with an attractive employee of the local saloon. Just as you notice what Mel is up to, you hear someone yelling. It's the sheriff's son, Pete, screaming furiously at Mel about tryin' to steal his gal. You can see the sun reflecting brightly from Pete's two chrome-plated Colts still in their holsters. A crowd is beginning to gather. . .

Gourmet Suspense

You have spent years decorating your home and updating your kitchen and dining area so you can entertain with the best. The local Society League is coming over for dinner and you've pulled out the stops. Even your family is cleaning up for the big event. Suddenly, before the guests arrive, your exuberant St. Bernard, Skipper, comes running into the kitchen after a dip in the pool. You face Skipper boldly as you quickly plan your next move. Too late. With what seems to be a smile, Skipper shakes himself indulgently and you watch in horror as water flies all over your kitchen and dog fur comes to rest gently all over your delicious food. The doorbell rings as your first guests arrive. . .

Executive Decision

You are the point person for talks between your company and a similar-sized competitor. They have proposed a merger and the deal looks good for everyone involved. Your boss, who is the CEO of your company, is behind you all the way and very proud of the work you have done on this deal. As an accountant from the other company rambles on about assets, capital and debt, you are half-heartedly scanning the proposal. Suddenly you notice some discrepancies in their offer. You focus your efforts on the details and discover that the value of their stock is grossly over-valued. You turn the page and realize that a sizable amount of leftover cash is earmarked for "Employee severance." As you feverishly shuffle through your notes it occurs to you that your company is being stolen and your own boss has a golden parachute! A voice interrupts your hectic thoughts. "Is everything alright?" your boss asks, smiling. . .

Undersea Adventure

It's about time! A leisurely vacation with your friends on a tranquil Caribbean island. You love the soft breezes and delicious seafood, but your real passion is scuba diving. As a matter of fact, you have offered to teach your friends how to scuba dive! You've shown them the basics in the hotel pool and on the last day you've rented a boat with all the necessary gear. You've decided to take them out to a coral reef about 5 miles from the shore. The dive is going great, considering everyone but you is a complete beginner. You're all swimming along together at a depth of 50 feet when you notice that some people are running low on air. You are still a good ways from the boat so you decide to head back. Suddenly, something catches your eye in the shifting sand 30 feet below you. It looks like the corner of a metal box. . . It's the sea chest from an ancient shipwreck! Your friends look at you anxiously as you seem to hesitate, and the sand may cover the chest completely at any moment. . .

Family Reunion

It's moments like this that make life worth-while. You have worked hard all your life to create a good home and good future for your children. You have tried to teach your family good values and strong faith. You've fixed their boo-boos, driven them to band practice, mended their hearts, played catch and even taken care of their children. The squeal of a child interrupts your reminiscing and you are reminded where you are. It's Christmas dinner, and the bountiful table is surrounded by your children, grandchildren and other relatives. You tap your glass with a spoon and the room gets ghostly quiet. You look at your spouse in the eye and then turn to the waiting faces of your family. "As your parents, we have an important announcement to make. . ."

The Blast-Off

Your friends called you a nerd when you told them you wanted to major in physics. Your parents were openly doubtful when you told them you wanted to go to graduate school. But everyone was proud when you got the job offer from NASA. Now, you've worked your way up the ladder and you are facing the greatest moment in your life. You are in mission control for the first manned launch to Mars. Sure there are 40 other people in mission control, but the excitement is exhilarating. As the countdown gets closer and closer to liftoff, you reflect on all the effort that has gone into this launch. Hundreds of people have devoted their lives to this project. The media has gone crazy. The entire nation sees this as the big chance for our country to prove themselves. After billions of dollars and countless congressional hearings the rocket is about to launch. Suddenly, a yellow light begins to blink on your control panel. A sensor is indicating a possible pressure problem in a navigational hydraulic system. Your data is unclear. It's your job to monitor this information. Do you alarm mission control and scrub the launch causing another delay, if not a complete scrub of the mission? Or do you hope it's not a serious problem? It could be nothing, or you could be blamed. The countdown continues, 10. . . 9. . . 8. . . The yellow light continues to blink. . .

Mutual Funds

You've just been given $10,000 to invest in various mutual funds. How much are you going to invest in each of the following funds?

_____**Aggressive Christian Growth:** This fund will give great returns to help me grow in my faith. The dividends include a greater love of God and a deeper commitment to my church.

_____**Fidelity Marriage Fund:** This fund will help ensure that my marriage is a wonderful loving relationship. The prospectus promises great communication and a wonderful family life.

_____**Balanced Time Fund:** This fund will help me budget my time effectively so my life is balanced. The broker says that this fund is a favorite of people who say they are too busy for the important things.

_____**Conservative Values Fund:** This fund will help my family return to the home-grown, traditional lifestyle of my ancestors. This fund includes such stocks as Honest Industries, Hard Work Mining, Family Products, and Patriots, Inc.

_____**Friendship Bond Fund:** Closer and deeper friendships is the pay-off of this fund. This fund boasts timeless dividends and wealth that "cannot be measured."

_____**Pacific/Caribbean Restoration Fund:** This fund will take you to exotic places for well-needed rest and relaxation. This is a good fund for someone who needs to spend a little on themselves.

_____**Security Rainy Day Fund:** This mutual fund promises to pay dividends for a rainy day. This fund is a safe hedge against any problem or disaster and will keep you from worrying about unexpected problems.

_____**Intelligent Strength Fund:** This is a fund especially designed for people who need to save money for college. Money invested in this fund will be ready to help a prospective student pay for tuition.

Twenty (Sharing) Questions (Part 2)

Here is a list of 20 sharing questions for groups that have been together for a few months. Choose one question for everyone to answer and take turns sharing why you answered the way you did.

- ❑ 1. Describe a time when "nature couldn't wait."

- ❑ 2. When is the first time you remember winning at something and how did it make you feel?

- ❑ 3. If you could pick one character in fiction, TV or the comics to identify with, who would that be and why?

- ❑ 4. What was the wildest prank you were ever involved in?

- ❑ 5. I am most like my mom in that I_____.

- ❑ 6. Do you like your name? If you could choose another name would would it be?

- ❑ 7. If you could do any job you wanted to, what would you be doing five years from now?

- ❑ 8. What is the best advice you've ever received?

- ❑ 9. What makes a home a home?

- ❑ 10. You are invisible for one day, what will you do?

- ❑ 11. Who is the most famous person you've ever met? How did it happen?

- ❑ 12. What would you have been voted "Most Likely to_____" while in high school?

- ❑ 13. Describe the circumstances around your first kiss.

- ❑ 14. You can raise one person from the dead. Who? Why?

- ❑ 15. What is your nickname? How did you get it?

- ❑ 16. What is your greatest accomplishment?

- ❑ 17. What do you think is the perfect age? Why?

- ❑ 18. Describe the most unforgettable character you have ever met.

- ❑ 19. What song reminds you of an incident in your life?

- ❑ 20. What place that you visited would you never visit again?

Fantasy Time

Four different fantasy situations. . . choose one and share your response to the situation with the group. Before you share your response, your group might choose to tell each other which fantasy you have chosen and let the group guess what your response might be before you share your answer.

You're sitting in your easy chair dozing in front of the TV when you hear the doorbell ring. You open the door to find the Publisher's Clearing House prize team. They hand you a bouquet of flowers, some balloons, and a check for $5,000,000!

What are you going to do with the money?

You are walking through a lush forest. You head toward a clearing, discovering a bright meadow and you see a man dressed in white, standing alone. You know instinctively that the person is an angel sent by God. He approaches you and says, "God has sent me to tell you his dreams for you."

What does he say?

You are surrounded by a huge choir. There is lightning, magnificent beasts, and stately men and women in white robes. A melodious, powerful voice echoes above you. You look up to see an awesome figure on a throne. You are in heaven! The voice says to you, "Well done, my good and faithful servant! Let me tell you why I am so proud of you!"

What does he say?

You are sitting in a large hall, the perfect setting for an awards banquet. Several people have been previously nominated for a prestigious award. The winner is announced and the crowd erupts in thunderous applause. You are speechless. You have won!

What award did you win? What reasons did the emcee give for your winning? What will you say in your acceptance speech?

People Pie

The people in our lives are one of our most precious resources. Of all the different relationships in your life, who gets the most of your time, your love, your energy?

You might use the Ice-Breaker called "My Roles" to remind you of the different ways people need your time, your energy, your love, your emotions, your creativity and your money.

Use the circles below to make pie charts which show who gets what from you.

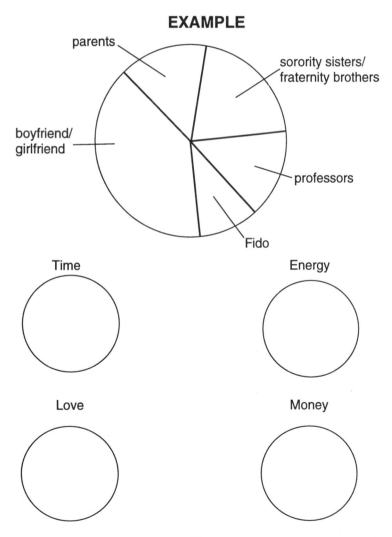

EXAMPLE

parents

sorority sisters/ fraternity brothers

boyfriend/ girlfriend

professors

Fido

Time

Energy

Love

Money

Ups and Downs

Our lives have their good times and their bad times. Help your group get to know you better by charting your life. From your birth to the present, mark the good times and bad times in your life. Feel free to explain some of these ups and downs to your group.

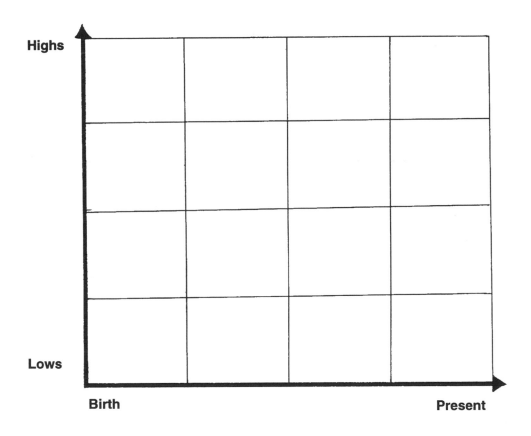

♥ : If your life is at a low point now, ask God for his help during your prayer time. If your life is at a high point now, be sure and thank God and ask him how you can use your situation to help others.

My Family

What was your family of origin like? Or what *is your* current family like? Help your small group understand your family. Select a movie, a fairy tale, nursery rhyme and a comic strip which best describes your family. Tell your group what you have chosen and feel free to explain your selections.

If my family was a movie, it would be. . .
- ❏ Nightmare on Elm Street
- ❏ The Parent Trap
- ❏ It's a Wonderful Life
- ❏ Home Alone
- ❏ Jurassic Park
- ❏ Pinocchio
- ❏ Parenthood
- ❏ Rambo
- ❏ Aladdin
- ❏ The Poseidon Adventure
- ❏ Star Wars
- ❏ Romeo and Juliet

If my family was a fairy tale, it would be. . .
- ❏ Hansel and Gretel
- ❏ Cinderella
- ❏ The Emperor's New Clothes
- ❏ Jack and the Beanstalk
- ❏ Sleeping Beauty
- ❏ The Pied Piper

If my family was a nursery rhyme, it would be. . .
- ❏ Old Woman Who Lived in a Shoe
- ❏ Old Mother Hubbard
- ❏ Little Miss Muffett
- ❏ Little Boy Blue
- ❏ Little Jack Horner
- ❏ Jack Spratt
- ❏ Humpty Dumpty
- ❏ Mary Had a Little Lamb

If my family was a comic strip, it would be. . .
- ❏ Blondie
- ❏ Peanuts
- ❏ Family Circus
- ❏ The Far Side
- ❏ Hagar the Horrible
- ❏ Andy Capp
- ❏ Calvin and Hobbes
- ❏ For Better, For Worse
- ❏ Dennis the Menace
- ❏ Outland
- ❏ B.C.
- ❏ Snuffy Smith

What I Need Right Now. . .

Choose five things from this list that you think you need more of. Tell the group why you chose what you did. (This list is adapted from *Structured Exercises in Wellness Promotion,* Tubesing and Tubesing, eds., Whole Person Press, 1983.)

vitality	self-esteem	direction
tenderness	composure	security
recognition	generosity	balance
activity	confidence	caring
awareness	health	motivation
sharing	solitude	devotion
contemplation	serenity	trust
insight	joy	commitment
communion	integration	forgiveness
surrender	faith	purpose
music	laughter	support
self-expression	companionship	harmony
romance	intimacy	patience
beauty	sensitivity	self-awareness
skill	opportunity	challenges
variety	structure	accomplishments
control	imagination	money
responsibility	education	experience
freedom	strength	energy
fitness	relaxation	comfort
nutrition	touching	sleep
childlikeness	coordination	flexibility
exercise	self-control	celebration

❤ Your group might wish to pray that each group member gets the things they need.

Real and Ideal

Use the chart below to describe the "real" status of several areas in your life. Then write down what the "ideal" status of these areas would be like. Choose 1 or 2 areas of your life and describe the real and ideal status to your group.

	Real	Ideal
Family Relationships		
Physical Health		
Spiritual Growth		
Career Goals		
Finances		
Love Life		

♥ : At the end of your meeting, choose one area of your life and tell the group how you plan on getting from the "real" to the "ideal." Pray and ask God to help you make the necessary changes.

Getting Older, Getting Better

Having more years under your belt means you are a wiser person. Answer the following questions about getting older and share your answers with the group.

Who was your childhood hero? Why? Who in the group demonstrates the qualities in the hero from your childhood? Answer these questions and share your answers with the group.

- ❑ Little Orphan Annie
- ❑ Shirley Temple
- ❑ An "Our Gang" character
- ❑ Laura Ingalls Wilder
- ❑ Nancy Drew
- ❑ Rebecca of Sunnybrook Farm
- ❑ Amelia Bedelia
- ❑ Curious George
- ❑ The Hardy Boys
- ❑ Peter Pan
- ❑ Superman
- ❑ Cap'n Crunch
- ❑ Davy Crockett
- ❑ Charles Lindberg
- ❑ H. R. Puffnstuff
- ❑ Johnny Quest
- ❑ Lou Gehrig
- ❑ Spiderman
- ❑ Michael Jordan
- ❑ Barney
- ❑ Batman
- ❑ Huck Finn
- ❑ Captain Marvel
- ❑ Babar the Elephant
- ❑ Larry Bird
- ❑ The president

"For mature adults, a small group is a good place to. . . "

- ❑ Play it safer
- ❑ Get more daring
- ❑ Get more serious
- ❑ Feel more content
- ❑ Worry more
- ❑ Have more regrets
- ❑ Laugh more
- ❑ Think more about the consequences
- ❑ Become more agreeable
- ❑ Think more about others
- ❑ Get grouchier
- ❑ Become more sentimental
- ❑ Get more eccentric
- ❑ Become more carefree
- ❑ Become more nostalgic
- ❑ Become less status conscious

What bugs me most about getting older is. . .

- ❑ having a fixed income when prices keep going up
- ❑ bifocals
- ❑ worrying about ill health
- ❑ not understanding today's music
- ❑ more aches, pains and stiffness
- ❑ inertia—my get up and go got up and went
- ❑ when people talk too loud to me

Self-Affirmation

Fill in the blanks and take turns telling your group about yourself.

My full name is. . .

I have. . . (two things you like about your appearance)

I take care of myself by. . . (one thing you do that is healthy)

At work, I am very good at. . . (two things you excel at on the job)

I contribute to a caring relationship by. . .
(one thing you do to maintain a good friendship)

When each person is finished sharing their answers about themselves, the rest of the group stands up and gives that person a standing ovation.

Snapshots

Let the group take a look at some interesting scenes from your past. Write down or draw the following snapshots of your life and tell your group about the most interesting ones.

A time I was really happy. . .

A time I toughed it out and accomplished my goal. . .

A time I took a big chance but it paid off. . .

A time I was real embarrassed. . .

A time I really chickened out. . .

A time I was really sad. . .

A 25-Hour Day?

How are you doing with time management? Consider the following lists of daily activities and answer the following questions:

Gardening	Sleeping
Cooking	Exercise
Work	Social engagements
Cleaning house	Trying to meet the right guy or girl
Overtime	Taking care of the kids
Church activities	Personal Devotional time
Rest	Hobbies:_____
Reading	Watching TV
Driving/Commuting	Getting dressed

If you are rushed for time, which of these things could you take out of your daily schedule?

If there were 25 hours in a day, what would you add to your daily schedule?

Your Doctor says "Slow Down!" How are you going to adjust your schedule to take it easy?

What's not in your daily schedule that needs to be?

Which activities constitute the most valuable use of your time?

Christian Basics, Part 1

How do you view the Christian faith? Answer these questions about different Christian topics and feel free to discuss your answers with your group. You may check more than one answer on each question.

This Ice-Breaker is intended to let people talk freely about their feelings on these religious subjects without worrying about "right or wrong" answers.

This is what I think about prayer
- ❑ wishful thinking
- ❑ direct line to God
- ❑ magic
- ❑ a life saver
- ❑ key to my sanity

- ❑ a psychological exercise
- ❑ powerful
- ❑ a daily practice
- ❑ positive thinking

I think of Jesus as. . .
- ❑ a great guy
- ❑ a wise teacher
- ❑ a miracle worker
- ❑ a Jewish rebel
- ❑ confused

- ❑ a courageous rabbi
- ❑ one of many teachers
- ❑ a great example
- ❑ a savior
- ❑ I'm not sure

I feel this way about church. . .
- ❑ scared
- ❑ boring
- ❑ friendly
- ❑ fun
- ❑ a fortress from the real world

- ❑ too traditional
- ❑ too hard to understand
- ❑ inspiring
- ❑ always asking for money
- ❑ confusing because of the different denominations

Most ministers are. . .
- ❑ wonderful people
- ❑ people like everyone else
- ❑ self-righteous
- ❑ under impossibly high expectations

- ❑ egocentric
- ❑ examples to follow
- ❑ too religious for the real world

Christian Basics, Part 2

Here are some more questions about the Christian faith. Remember, the purpose is not to give "right" or "wrong" answers, but to share your feelings honestly with your group. Answer the questions about these different Christian topics and share your answers with the group.

I think this about the Bible. . .

- ❏ Hard to read
- ❏ Inspiring
- ❏ Hard to apply
- ❏ Full of violence
- ❏ Too far-removed from our culture
- ❏ Old-fashioned
- ❏ Full of promises
- ❏ Secret to life
- ❏ Too many pages

This is what I think about Christians. . .

- ❏ Salt of the earth
- ❏ Too conservative
- ❏ World-changers
- ❏ More loving
- ❏ Too extreme
- ❏ Hypocrites
- ❏ Just like everyone else
- ❏ God's people
- ❏ Pollyanna

This is how I feel about small groups. . .

- ❏ Too touchy-feely
- ❏ Trendy
- ❏ Inspiring
- ❏ Prying
- ❏ Biblical
- ❏ Frightening
- ❏ What God intended
- ❏ Too much time out of my week

When I think about the cross I feel. . .

- ❏ Squeamish
- ❏ Humble
- ❏ Relieved
- ❏ Unsure
- ❏ Nothing
- ❏ Inspired
- ❏ Hopeful
- ❏ Skeptical
- ❏ Angry

Under the Big Top

Look at the picture of the circus. If you imagine your family as a circus, which performers represent members of your family? If your small group was a circus, which performer would you be? Share your answers with your group.

Family Connections

Talking about your family with your small group is a good way for everyone in the group to understand each other. In the space below draw a circle for each one of your current family members, or your family members when you were a child. (Include relatives, step-brothers, step-sisters, and step-parents if you want to). Write each person's name inside each circle.

Next, draw a solid line between people in your family who care about each other. Draw a dotted line between family members who are ambivalent about each other. Draw a jagged line between family members who do not get along. Draw a wavy line between yourself and a family member you really admire.

Past, Present, Future

A small group is a good place to "be yourself." Being yourself means freely discussing your past, present and future. A "Past, Present and Future" Ice-Breaker helps group members discuss their life in a comprehensive way.

PAST: If I were young again, I would spend more time. . .
- ❏ Reading great books
- ❏ Praying
- ❏ Talking about_____
- ❏ Playing
- ❏ Spending time with my family
- ❏ Making my community a better place
- ❏ Getting involved in church
- ❏ Stopping to smell the flowers
- ❏ Loving my friends

PRESENT: Life would be a better place if there were more. . .
- ❏ Parades
- ❏ Family picnics
- ❏ Country fairs
- ❏ Carnivals and circuses
- ❏ Sunday dinners
- ❏ Revivals
- ❏ Corner druggists
- ❏ Mom and Pop stores
- ❏ Homemade bread
- ❏ Square dances
- ❏ Easter egg hunts

FUTURE: When I am 100 years old, I hope I am still able to. . .
- ❏ Make love
- ❏ Drive a car
- ❏ Grow flowers
- ❏ Take care of myself
- ❏ Play with children
- ❏ Walk a mile
- ❏ Make people laugh
- ❏ Play basketball
- ❏ Go on a date
- ❏ Listen to rock music
- ❏ Take a joke
- ❏ Earn a living
- ❏ Think creatively

A Self Description

There are 300 words listed here in alphabetical order. Choose one word that starts with each letter of your name. For example, if your name is Joe, you might choose "jolly," "optimistic," and "exhausted." Share your self description with your group members. Before you do, you might wish to let your group choose words which they think describe you. (This list is adapted from *Structured Experiences in Wellness Promotion,* edited by Tubseling and Tubseling, Whole Person Press, 1983.)

accepting	calm	embarrassed	guilty
admirable	cared for	envious	
adored	cautious	esteemed	happy
affectionate	cocky	exasperated	hateful
aggravated	comfortable	excited	helpless
alert	competent	exhausted	hopeful
amazed	concerned	expectant	hopeless
ambivalent	confident		horrified
amusing	confused	faithful	hostile
angry	courageous	fearful	humbled
annoyed	curious	fed up	humiliated
anxious	cynical	fond	hurt
appalled		forlorn	
appreciated	daring	frantic	impatient
ashamed	dejected	friendly	important
assured	delighted	frightened	idolized
astonished	dependent	frustrated	inadequate
awed	depressed	fulfilled	independent
	desperate	furious	indifferent
bashful	disappointed		indignant
benevolent	discouraged	glad	infatuated
bewildered	dismayed	gleeful	inferior
bitter	dissatisfied	gloomy	inhibited
bold	doubtful	good	inquisitive
bored		grateful	insecure
buoyant	eager	great	irritated
brave	edgy	grieved	
bright	egregious	grouchy	jealous
burned out	elated	grumpy	jittery
			jocular

jolly
jumpy

kaleidoscopic
keen
kicky
killjoy
kind
kingly
knocked down
knowing

lethargic
lionlike
listless
lively
loathed
lonely
longing
lost
loved
loyal

mad
majestic
meaningless
melancholy
methodical
mind-boggling
mischievous
miserable
moody
motherly
mourning
multifaceted

naive
natural

needy
nervous
newsworthy
nostalgic
notable

off-the-wall
old-fashioned
on-track
optimistic
out of place
overwhelmed

pained
panicky
passionate
patient
peaceful
perplexed
pessimistic
pitiful
pleased
pressured
proud
provoked
puzzled

quaint
questioning
quick
quiet
quotable

refreshed
regretful
rejected
relaxed
relieved

reluctant
repulsed
resentful
resigned
restless
risking

sad
satisfaction
scared
self-confident
self-conscious
shocked
shy
skeptical
solemn
sorry
startled
strong
stubborn
supported
surprised
sympathetic

tender
tense
tempted
threatened
thrilled
timid
tough
tranquil
trapped
troubled
trusting

uncomfortable
understanding

uneasy
unflappable
unflinching
unfulfilled
unhappy
unobtrusive
unsure
untroubled
upbeat
uproarious
upset
uptight

valiant
valued
vibrant
vital
vulnerable

warm
weak
weary
whimsical
wonderful
worn out
worried
worthless
worthy
wounded

yearning
young-at-heart

zany
zealous
zesty
zoned-out

A Slice of Life

As you think about all the different things you do in your life, do you consider your time well managed? How much of your time is spent at:

work
sleep
play
church
driving
cleaning
cooking
caring for others
etc.

Draw a pie chart which shows how your time is spent right now. Draw another pie chart which shows your "fantasy life." Finally, draw a third pie chart which shows an ideal balance between your current situation and your dream life.

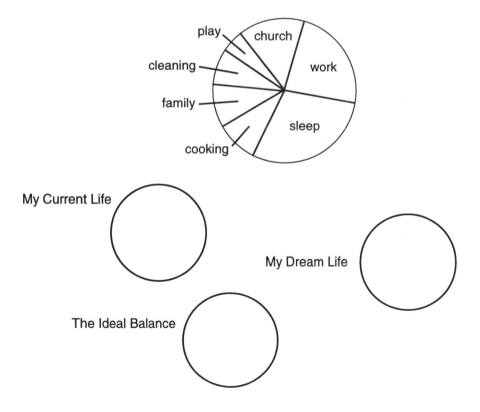

My Stock Market

Pretend you are a publicly owned national corporation. Something like "Bob, Inc." Who are your stockholders? Who has invested in you? Who would suffer the most if your "company" filed Chapter 11? Who would strike it rich if your stock shot up after a 3 for 1 split?

You've offered an initial release of 1000 shares of your stock. Using a list of all the people who own "stock" in you, write their names and how many shares each person owns. Tell your group who owns your stock.

_____, my spouse/significant other, _____ shares

_____, my place of work, _____ shares

_____, my children, _____ shares

_____, my parents, _____ shares

_____, a friend, _____ shares

_____, a friend, _____ shares

_____, my hobby, _____ shares

_____, my pet, _____ shares

Magic Treasure Chest

Giving gifts is a great expression of love and familiarity. Answer the following questions about gifts you have given and received.

The best gift I ever got was. . .

The best gift I ever gave was. . .

How I feel when I get something. . .

How I feel when I give something. . .

When you are finished with the questions, trade booklets with another group member and write in the name of the gift you would like to give that person if you could give them anything in the world. Be sure and fill out the tag so they know who gave it to them!

Milestones

For many of us, our lives are marked by important transitions. A powerful meeting with God, a major decision, a marrlage proposal, an important accomplishment, a conversion experience or any profound event. Where were you when these life-changing events took place?

In the three boxes below, draw or describe where you were when you passed the most important milestones in your life.

Power People

Some people are more than just people. There are people in your life that have a powerful effect on you. The different types of "power people" are listed below. In the blanks list the family and friends who are the "power people" in your life.

_____ **Listener.** The person who is always there to hear what I have to say without trying to change me.

_____ **Challenger.** That special person who has a way of bringing out the best in me, even when I'm complacent.

_____ **Devil's Advocate.** One of those people who love me enough to tell me things I might not want to hear.

_____ **Encourager.** Someone who has a way of keeping me looking on the bright side of things.

_____ **Prayer Partner.** Someone I trust enough to come with me when I go to God in prayer.

_____ **Role Model.** The kind of person I want to emulate in my actions, character, and reputation.

_____ **Mentor.** One of those people who is willing to take me under their wing and guide me on my life's journey.

_____ **Inspire.** That wonderful type of person who can elevate my spirit and remind me that God has everything in control.

_____ **Consoler.** The person who can calm me down when life gets out of control.

_____ **Playmate.** Someone who I can always count on to do something fun and bring out the child in me.

_____ **Dream Partner.** That special person who will listen to and appreciate my dreams.

♥ At the end of your meeting, you could use this Ice-Breaker as an affirmation exercise. For each of these "power people" fill in the name of a group member who is that person in your life or someone you can imagine being that person in your life.

Precious Time

God has given us a precious gift: the time to live. Maybe that's why now is called "the present . . ."

Answer the following three questions about precious time. After you answer the questions, tell your answers to the group.

My idea of a great time is. . .
- ❑ A quiet evening at home
- ❑ Watching movies
- ❑ A hot bath after a long day
- ❑ Good book in front of fireplace
- ❑ A delicious meal
- ❑ A fun night out with the gang
- ❑ A brisk walk on a fall afternoon
- ❑ A day shopping with friends
- ❑ Hard work that pays off
- ❑ Watch an exciting sports event

These things make a bad day for me. . .
- ❑ Rainy weather
- ❑ Mondays
- ❑ Emotional swings
- ❑ Paying bills
- ❑ Boring work
- ❑ Traffic
- ❑ Conflict
- ❑ Hot, humid afternoons
- ❑ Lousy financial news

If I knew I had six months to live, I would. . .
- ❑ Do exactly what I'm doing now
- ❑ See the world
- ❑ Write my memoirs
- ❑ Finish my "Big Project"
- ❑ Give everything away
- ❑ Be very angry
- ❑ Love everyone more
- ❑ Climb Mt. Everest

High Anxiety

A small group is a great place to share the burden of your anxieties with people who care about you. The grid below will help you distinguish between anxieties that you can and cannot control.

Here is a partial listing of things in our lives which can cause anxiety and stress:

Financial problems	Marital conflict	Teenagers
Work issues	Taxes	World events
Medical problems	Moving	Stock market
Real estate	Bills	Loneliness

Think of the anxieties which you face in your life right now. Using the chart below, write your anxieties in the appropriate quadrant. Some anxieties are high, some are low. Some anxieties can be controlled, some cannot.

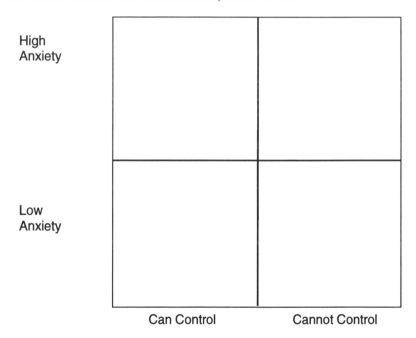

After you have written down your anxieties, tell the group what anxieties you put in each quadrant.

♥ It would be a good idea to close your meeting with the Serenity prayer or its equivalent. This involves asking God to take away your anxiety for things you cannot control, assistance with distinguishing between low anxieties and high anxieties, and help in finding solutions and a sense of peace for the concerns you can control.

Money and Success

Paul said that "the love of money is the root of all evil." There is no doubt that money can play a powerful role in our life. The same is true for success.

Your group can learn a lot about each other by discussing your answers to these questions about money and success.

My idea about money is. . .
- ❏ It's a frustrating burden
- ❏ It should be saved
- ❏ Spend, spend, spend!
- ❏ Something I need more of
- ❏ It's a necessary evil
- ❏ A source of arguments
- ❏ A source of fun
- ❏ Like always playing catch up
- ❏ It's a resource for freedom

My advice to anyone who wants to get ahead. . .
- ❏ Set specific goals
- ❏ Don't worry about people's feelings
- ❏ Forget it
- ❏ Keep a balanced life instead
- ❏ Don't neglect your family
- ❏ It's not worth it
- ❏ Doesn't mean you're a better person
- ❏ Sentimentality and principles are liabilities
- ❏ Damn the torpedoes, full speed ahead!

My idea of someone who is a success is. . .
- ❏ Mother Theresa
- ❏ Martin Luther King, Jr.
- ❏ Donald Trump
- ❏ Ghandi
- ❏ George Washington Carver
- ❏ Wayne Gretzky
- ❏ The President
- ❏ Norman Rockefeller
- ❏ Ludwig von Beethoven
- ❏ Elizabeth Taylor
- ❏ Hank Aaron

Improvements

All of us have relationships we need to improve. Talking about these needed changes with other people can prompt us to action, when keeping it to ourselves might not lead to the necessary changes.

Using the list below, write down the names of people you are in relationship with. Then write down how you can improve those relationships. Share your plan of action with your group.

The relationship I need to improve is. . .

My spouse:_____

My parents: _____

My child:_____

My boss:_____

A co-worker:_____

A friend: _____

A church member: _____

A sibling: _____

A relative: _____

An old flame: _____

Other: _____

How I plan on improving this relationship is. . .

♥ During your prayer time you might ask God to help you make the necessary changes to make your relationships better.

Family Traits

Our family background is an important factor determining who we are. Your small group will learn a lot about you as they learn more about your family.

Answer the following questions about your family and share them with your group.

I feel like my parents look upon me as. . .

- ❏ a troublesome kid
- ❏ a scapegoat
- ❏ a security blanket
- ❏ their pride and joy
- ❏ a disappointment
- ❏ a wonderful person
- ❏ a continuation of themselves

- ❏ a helpless baby
- ❏ glue
- ❏ a capable adult
- ❏ a liability
- ❏ invisible
- ❏ good stock
- ❏ the family name

I feel like my children see me as. . . (Or I look upon my parents as. . .)

- ❏ a role model
- ❏ their enemy
- ❏ a pushover
- ❏ the great provider
- ❏ a household slave
- ❏ source of love

- ❏ a complete fool
- ❏ a friend
- ❏ a bag of money
- ❏ godlike
- ❏ a chauffeur

I feel like my parents expect me to be. . .

- ❏ the next president
- ❏ an incredible success
- ❏ completely obedient
- ❏ the next Albert Einstein
- ❏ a golden boy/girl
- ❏ independent
- ❏ a compensation for their failures
- ❏ whatever makes me happy

- ❏ a doctor
- ❏ a minister
- ❏ just like them
- ❏ perfect
- ❏ a princess
- ❏ self-sufficient

Getting Older, Getting Better, #2

Looking back on your life is a valuable exercise small group members can share together.

Answer these questions and take turns sharing your responses with the group.

One thing I really miss is. . .

❏ coal furnaces
❏ outhouses
❏ PF Flyers
❏ homemade ice cream
❏ model "T" cars
❏ milk at the door
❏ making jelly
❏ recess

❏ picking vegetables
❏ coonskin caps
❏ safe streets
❏ wool long johns
❏ crew cuts
❏ porch swings
❏ playing kickball
❏ watching cartoons

If I had my choice, I would rather spend my last years. . .

❏ in a retirement community
❏ seeing the country in a motor home
❏ on my motorcycle
❏ at my very own house
❏ playing golf
❏ with my children
❏ working hard at my job
❏ writing a great novel
❏ dancing every night
❏ meeting new challenges
❏ giving back to my community

A dream I've always had that I look forward to fulfilling in the future is. . .

❏ write a book
❏ serving in the Peace Corp
❏ do something positive in my community
❏ operating my own art studio
❏ contribute to the efforts of my church
❏ learn something new:_____
❏ run for office
❏ invent something:_____

Emotional Dashboard

How are you feeling? Let's check your gauges on the emotional dashboard. Use the drawing below to mark where you are emotionally. Is your fuel tank of compassion full or empty? How many miles per hour is your enthusiasm running? How about your stress pressure?

Fill in the gauges below and take turns sharing with your group how you are feeling.

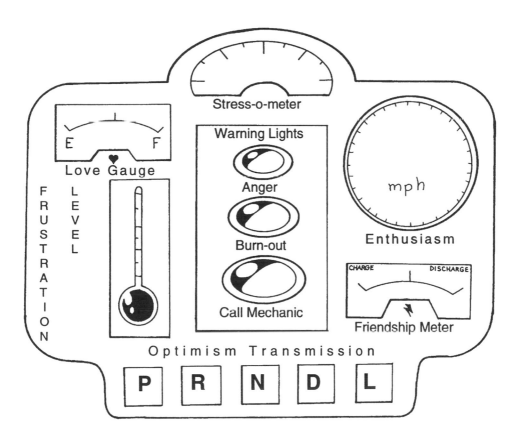

Who's It Gonna Be?

Write down the name of a friend you would choose to join you in the following activities. Why would you choose this person? You can also play this game by choosing which family member or relative you would choose to do these things.

_____ **Go fishing.** A wonderful, peaceful afternoon by the water, talking softly and bragging about "the big one that got away."

_____ **Pray.** An activity to be shared with someone with a deep faith and a trustful heart.

_____ **Go shopping.** It's fun to walk around with a friend and look into store windows and buy the perfect item. This is going to be a busy day so put on your walking shoes!

_____ **Get stuck on a deserted island.** For an adventure like this you'll need someone who is crafty and resourceful, who is also a great companion, easy to get along with.

_____ **Eat sushi.** Who would you choose to go eat something new and different? If not sushi, try mountain oysters, pig knuckles or calf sweetbreads.

_____ **Talk about my problems.** A task like this requires someone who is sympathetic, compassionate and understanding. You do not want someone who will pass judgment, but will listen intently.

_____ **Cry with.** When you are at your most vulnerable, you need a special companion who is nurturing and protective.

_____ **Go to Disneyland.** It's a great trip to a giant playground! You will want to take someone who is fun, childlike and daring.

_____ **Talk about God.** When discussing deep spiritual truths, you want to talk with someone who has an accurate, positive understanding of God.

♥ If your group has gotten to know each other fairly well, write down the name of the group member you can imagine doing a particular activity in the space next to that activity. Tell the group why you chose each person with that particular activity.

Twenty (sharing) Questions, Part 3

These Sharing Questions should be used for groups that have been together for several months. Take turns answering these questions and discussing your answers.

- ❑ 1. What do you like most about yourself?
- ❑ 2. What one blessing have you received from this group?
- ❑ 3. Has there been a situation recently where you were instrumental in the growth of another person? What did you do?
- ❑ 4. If you could wave a magic wand and make your job or marriage or church or family perfect, how would it be different than it is now? What is one thing you could do this week to move toward those changes?
- ❑ 5. What do you need to do to make your Christian life more meaningful and effective?
- ❑ 6. If you could live a year of your life over again, which year would you choose? Why?
- ❑ 7. If you had to describe one frustration you've had with this group, what would it be?
- ❑ 8. If given a choice, how would you choose to die? How do you not want to die?
- ❑ 9. If you were to describe yourself as a flavor, what would your flavor be?
- ❑ 10. Where do you go or what do you do when life gets too heavy? Why do you do this?
- ❑ 11. For what in your life are you most grateful?
- ❑ 12. What was your most embarrassing moment?
- ❑ 13. Share a memory of your grandmother or grandfather.
- ❑ 14. What qualities do you prize most in a friend?
- ❑ 15. In what way are you different from the way people usually see you?
- ❑ 16. If you knew you could not fail, what are two things that you would like to accomplish?
- ❑ 17. When was the first time you heard about Jesus and what did you think about him?
- ❑ 18. When, if ever, did God become more than just a word to you?
- ❑ 19. What three things do you like/dislike about your father?
- ❑ 20. What three things do you like/dislike about your mother?

What Time Is It?

Answer this question by drawing in the hands on this clock: "What time is it in my life? Why?" Then answer the questions at the bottom of the page. When everyone has finished share your answers with the group.

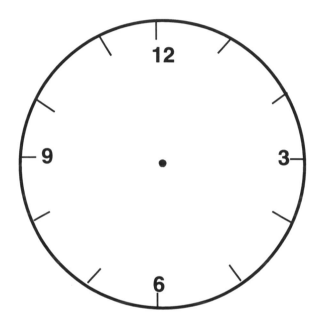

It's almost time for:

It's too late for:

When it is _____ o'clock, I'll:

"How Can We Pray For You?" (Part 1)

Here are some recommended ways for a small group to pray together. These methods are especially valuable for those groups that are new together, new to a small group, or new to the whole concept of prayer.

The prayer time can be the most powerful portion of a small group meeting. After an Ice-Breaker and a safe period of study and discussion, the final portion of your meeting can be the most meaningful moments of the week. A loving, accepting group of people who pray together can open hearts and change lives in extraordinary ways.

There are many ways a small group can pray together. These ways have been divided according to how long the group has been together. Use one of the following methods of prayer to close your group meeting.

1. Let your leader close the group in prayer as he or she sees fit. Typically, the leader will thank God for the opportunity to meet together, offer praise and thanks to God, pray for situations in anyone's life that might have been mentioned during the meeting, and ask God's help in applying the message(s) of the meeting lesson or discussion.

2. Read a prayer out loud together, such as the Lord's prayer, or the Serenity prayer. Make sure everyone has a copy!

   The Lord's Prayer:

   "Our Father in heaven, hallowed be your name. Your kingdom come. Your will be done, on earth as it is in heaven. Give us this day our daily bread. And forgive us our debts, as we also have forgiven our debtors. And do not bring us to the time of trial, but deliver us from the evil one. For the kingdom and the power and the glory are yours forever. Amen!"

The Serenity Prayer:

"God, grant us the serenity to accept the things that we cannot control, the courage to change the things we can, and the wisdom to now the difference. Amen!"

3. Let the leader close in prayer, but ask each group member to pray for the group during the week. This involves each group member spending a few minutes alone during the coming week talking to God about the group. Praying for the group can include thanking God for the opportunity to get to know the people in the group, praying for specific people and the issues in their lives, and praying that the group continue to become a growing, caring family.

Pick a Promise

Take your pick. Read over the list of special promises in scripture listed below and check the one you want for the days ahead. Tell the group why you chose the one you did.

You can also personalize the promise. After you have chosen a verse, restate it in personal language. For example, if you personalized the first verse listed below, it would sound like this: "Therefore, if I am in Christ, I am a new creation: the old has gone, the new has come!"

"Therefore, if anyone is in Christ, he is a new creation; the old has gone, the new has come!" 2 Corinthians 5:17

". . . being confident of this, that he who began a good work in you will carry it on to completion until the day of Christ Jesus." Philippians 1:6

"Call to me, and I will answer you; I will tell you wonderful and marvelous things that you know nothing about." Jeremiah 33:3

"And God is able to make all grace abound to you, so that in all things at all times having all that you need, you will abound in every good work." 2 Corinthians 9:8

"I can do everything through him who gives me strength." Philippians 4:13

"And we know that in all things God works for the good of those who love him, who have been called according to his purpose." Romans 8:28

"Ask and it will be given to you; seek and you will find; knock and the door will be opened to you. For everyone who asks receives; he who seeks finds; and to him who knocks, the door will be opened." Matthew 7:7-8

"No temptation has seized you except what is common to man. And God is faithful; he will not let you be tempted beyond what you can bear. But when you are tempted, he will also provide a way out so that you can stand up under it." 1 Corinthians 10:13

"Here I am! I stand at the door and knock. If anyone hears my voice and opens the door, I will come in and eat with him, and he with me." Revelation 3:20

The Lord's Prayer

When Jesus was asked, "How should we pray?" he gave us the Lord's Prayer. Use the Lord's Prayer as a model as your group writes their own prayer.

There are two options for this Heart-Warmer. One option is assign each line of the Lord's Prayer to one of your group members. Each group member restates that line of the Lord's Prayer in their own words. The group closes in prayer by going around the group and letting each group member read their line of the prayer.

Another option is to ask each group member to restate the entire prayer. The group closes by letting any willing group member share their own version of the Lord's Prayer.

"Our Father

in heaven,

hallowed be your name.

Your kingdom come.

Your will be done,

on earth as it is in heaven.

Give us this day our daily bread.

And forgive us our debts,

as we also have forgiven our debtors.

And do not bring us to the time of trial,

but deliver us from the evil one.

For the kingdom and the power and the glory are yours forever. Amen."

You Remind Me Of. . .

Write your name on a slip of paper and put it in a hat. Let everyone in the group select a name from the hat. Select a building, a work of art and weather which describes the person you have chosen.

When everyone is finished, read out loud the particular building, work of art and weather you selected and see if the group can guess who you are describing.

BUILDINGS

YELLOWSTONE LODGE
You are stately and rustic, a solidly built unpretentious place for people to find rest while on their grand adventure.

U.N. BUILDING
You are an inspiring place of peace and cooperation. People from everywhere look to you for guidance.

MAGNIFICENT SKYSCRAPER
You keep us looking upward! You soar into the sky as you rise above other buildings. You can see for miles from your heights.

THE LOUVRE
You are full of creativity and masterpieces. Anyone who sees what you have inside is stunned by the beauty.

RESORT HOTEL
People come to you to recuperate and escape the pressures of their lives. You offer thoughtful hospitality and comfortable luxury.

PAGODA
You are an inscrutable mystery and you emanate exotic, mysteriousness and peaceful harmony.

GINGERBREAD HOUSE
You are the sweetest! A magical place of delightful treats freely given to anyone who discovers your surprises.

ROSE BOWL
You are a place people go to celebrate and have a good time!

FORT KNOX
You are a strong vault, full of precious treasures. Most people can hardly imagine the value of what you contain.

ST PATRICK'S CATHEDRAL
When people are near you they have a sense of being on holy ground.

WEATHER

RAINBOW
You show the full spectrum of God's creation as you light up a stormy sky with your hopeful colors.

BRIGHT SUMMER DAY
With a clear sky full of a warm, radiant sun, you encourage everyone to go outside, get active and play!

SUNSET
You shine bright colors across the world, showing everyone that even though night is coming there is plenty of beauty in the world.

GENTLE SNOWFALL
By covering everything with a pure white blanket, you remind everyone what a holy place the world can be.

SHOOTING STAR
You light up the starry sky with a dazzling display, reminding everyone that heaven is full of brilliant surprises.

CRACKLING LIGHTNING
Your power and energy are seen by people everywhere.

SPRING SHOWER
A refreshing rainfall, you nourish the world and bring new growth from everything you touch.

DRENCHING RAIN
Wherever you go people are soaked in nourishment and feel refreshed and ready to grow.

COOL FRONT
When the heat has sapped everyone's strength, you blow in to make everyone feel refreshed and revitalized.

FULL MOON
In the darkest night you are there shining brightly and taking away the fear.

WORKS OF ART

MONA LISA
Your warm, enigmatic smile
reminds everyone who looks
at you of the mystical and
and mysterious side of life.

APPALACHIAN WOOD CARVING
Your down-to-earth style and
uncomplicated beauty show us that
the simple things of life are the most
precious.

REMINGTON BRONZE
You are durable and hardy,
reminding everyone of the
rip-snorting days of the old
west.

MONET'S WATER LILIES
Your soft colors and tranquil scenes
have given us the lasting impression
of someone who is gentle and
expressive.

GREEK STATUE
You embody the beauty of the
classic spirit, possessing
virtues which have been
cherished for centuries.

A CHILD'S FINGERPAINTING
It's bright colors and fun! Your
childlike nature makes everyone
smile.

PICASSO PAINTING
You are exotic and unique,
showing us a side of life that
we have never seen before,
but love to look at.

CALDER MOBILE
You seem to float with an innate
grace and balance, giving those
around you a flowing sense of calm.

RODIN'S "THE THINKER"
Your deep intelligence is a mon-
umental encouragement to all
of us to respect our ability to find
answers and solve problems.

BOTTICELLI'S "BIRTH OF VENUS"
You seem to epitomize the
renaissance spirit of a rich life and
a keen awareness of the natural
world.

Have Hope!

Here is a collection of Bible verses on the subject of hope. Choose one that best speaks to your situation, read it to the group, and tell them why you chose it.

"Why are you downcast, O my soul? Why so disturbed within me? Put your hope in God, for I will yet praise him, my Savior and my God."   Psalm 42:11

"Therefore, prepare your minds for action; be self-controlled, set your hope fully on the grace to be given you when Jesus Christ is revealed."   1 Peter 1:13

"The faith and love that spring from the hope that is stored up for you in heaven and that you have already heard about in the word of truth, the gospel."
Colossians 1:5

"Be strong and take heart, all you who hope in the Lord."   Psalm 31:24

"For you have been my hope, O Sovereign Lord, my confidence since my youth."
Psalm 71:5

"Praise be to the God and Father of our Lord Jesus Christ! In his great mercy he has given us new birth into a living hope through the resurrection of Jesus Christ from the dead."   1 Peter 1:3

"Let us hold unswervingly to the hope we profess, for he who promised is faithful."
Hebrews 10:23

"Know therefore that the Lord your God is God; he is the faithful God, keeping his covenant of love to a thousand generations of those who love him and keep his commands."   Deuteronomy 7:9

"And if the Spirit of him who raised Jesus from the dead is living in you, he who raised Christ from the dead will also give life to your mortal bodies through his Spirit, who lives in you."   Romans 8:11

"He will wipe every tear from their eyes. There will be no more death or mourning or crying or pain, for the old order of things has passed away."
Revelation 21:4

"Now we know that if the earthly tent we live in is destroyed, we have a building from God, an eternal house in heaven, not built by human hands."
2 Corinthians 5:1

Progressive Poetry

How would you like to write a poem about your small group? First, your group needs to choose between word group #1, #2 or #3. Next, everyone in your group needs to choose one of the words in that word group. Then, have everyone in your group write a sentence explaining what they like about the group. This sentence should have 8-10 syllables and end with the word they have chosen. Finally, go around the group and take turns reading your sentences. The result should be a wonderful poem about your group!

Word Group #1	Word Group #2	Word Group #3
I	way	free
sky	say	be
hi	stay	see
pie	today	thee
why	okay	tea
my	may	bee
by	day	she
fly	pay	he
try	hey	we
shy	bay	me
	clay	glee
	pray	spree

You can also try various options of this Ice-Breaker. For example, if there are 8 people in your group, choose 4 words, such as "pie," "clay," "free," and "jack." Have two people write an 8-10 syllable sentence that rhymes with "pie," 2 other people write a sentence rhyming with "clay," etc. When everyone has finished their sentences, collect them, sort them, and read the finished product to the group.

Here is an example of a progressive poem written by the Guacamole group in Austin, Texas.

> We have fun as we eat and talk and play,
> Thank God it's time to play and pray!
>
> We go deep inside and then we get high,
> The group that never fails to try and try.
>
> For warm ideas we seldom lack,
> and it seems they always want to come back.
>
> You've helped me discover how to just be,
> A chance to talk, to share, to bond, to be. . .

Everyday Blessings

Have everyone in your group think about the person on their left. Choose an everyday object that reminds you of a special quality possessed by that person. You might choose a lightbulb because that person lights up the room, or you might choose the paper clip because that person holds the group together. Use one of the examples shown below or come up with your own ideas.

When everyone is ready, tell your person what you selected and why it reminds you of them.

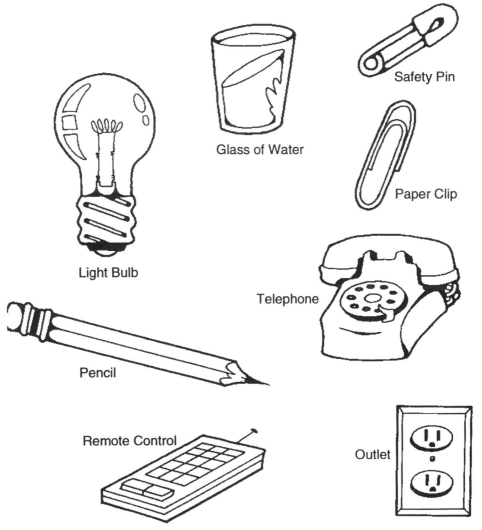

Glass of Water

Safety Pin

Paper Clip

Light Bulb

Telephone

Pencil

Remote Control

Outlet

"How Can We Pray For You?" (Part 2)

When the group is more comfortable with one another, they can begin praying in different ways. Remember, no one should pray out loud if they do not want to. Prayer should never be coerced or cause someone to feel uncomfortable.

These methods of small group prayer suggest that the leader of the group do most of the "out loud" prayer. However, the leader might ask if anyone else in the group would be willing to pray.

1. Let those group members who are willing share their prayer concerns with the group. The leader can close the meeting by praying for these concerns. This involves sharing "prayer requests" or "prayer concerns." A prayer request is when you tell someone about something you would like them to pray about, such as a job interview, a sick child, or the opportunity to share Christ with a co-worker. Remember that advice-giving is not appropriate during the prayer request time.

   In this case, your leader might ask, "How can we pray for you this week," or "Does anyone have any prayer requests?" Then the group can take turns sharing those concerns in their lives that they would like other group members to pray about during the week. A valuable opportunity for sharing prayer requests is to share those concerns that were brought to mind during the Bible study and discussion portion of the meeting.

2. After prayer requests have been shared, ask each group member to pray for the concerns of another group member during the coming week. This can be done by having each person pray for the person (and their concerns) sitting on their right or left. "Prayer partners" can also be used. Group members are paired up and pray for each other during the coming week. The leader, or someone else who would like to, can close the meeting in prayer.

3. After prayer requests have been made, ask each group member to pray for the person on the right or left "silently." The leader can begin this period of silent prayer and close the prayer time by praying out loud.

God Is In Control (Thank Goodness)

God is in control! Sometimes we get stressed out because we worry about things that God is taking care of. Pick one of these verses which reminds you that God is in control. Read your verse to the group and tell them why you chose it. Personalizing verses like this can be helpful. This involves restating the verse as though it was written to you personally. For example, if you personalized the first verse on the list, it would sound like this: "I will cast all my anxiety on him because he cares for me."

"Cast all your anxiety on him because he cares for you."   *1 Peter 5:7*

"Do not be afraid little flock, for your Father has been pleased to give you the kingdom."   *Luke 12:32*

"Trust in the Lord with all your heart and lean not on your own understanding; in all your ways acknowledge him, and he will make your paths straight."   *Proverbs 3:5-6*

"God is our refuge and strength, an ever present help in trouble. Therefore we will not fear, though the earth give way and the mountains fall into the heart of the sea."   *Psalm 46:1-2*

"If you make the Most High your dwelling—even the Lord, who is my refuge— then no harm will befall you, no disaster will come near your tent."   *Psalm 91:9-10*

"I will lie down and sleep in peace, for you alone, O Lord, make me dwell in safety."   *Psalm 4:8*

"The Lord will keep you from all harm—he will watch over your life, the Lord will watch over your coming and going both now and forevermore."   *Psalm 121:7-8*

"Let the beloved of the Lord rest secure in him, for he shields him all day long, and the one the Lord loves rests between his shoulders."   *Deuteronomy 33:12*

"The Lord is my rock, my fortress and my deliverer; my God is my rock, in whom I take refuge. He is my shield and the horn of my salvation, my stronghold."   *Psalm 18:2*

"I have told you these things, so that in me you may have peace. In this world you will have trouble. But take heart! I have overcome the world."   *John 16:33*

Go Ahead and Ask!

Asking God for something is an important type of prayer. This can be a prayer for yourself or on behalf of someone else. Use the list below to help you decide what to pray about. You could also use this list to let each group member lead a prayer on certain topics. One group member could pray for those who are sick, based on the prayer concerns about illness other group members have shared. Another group member could pray for the community, or the church, or family members, etc.

Your group can also refer to this list regularly to help assure that prayers are being offered by your group on behalf of those who need them.

Ourselves, such as. . .
relationships	money	personal growth
crisis	health	self-control

Our small group, including. . .
building community   choosing a mission or task
deciding what to study next   finding new group members

Our families. . .
improving communication	raising children	getting along
building trust	making a decision	loving each other

Our church, such as. . .
leadership	evangelism	helping less fortunate
worship services	certain programs	finances
building program	new members	youth and children

The government, including. . .
city government	county government	state government
federal government	particular legislation	community leaders
congressional representatives		

Those without Christ. . .
Christ-less friends   people who feel unloved
countries and regions without churches

Our society, including. . .
moral problems	crime	poverty	purposelessness
unemployment	youth	violence	inflation

Our world. . .
war	famine	environmental problems
oppression	economic issues	prejudice

Thanks Bunches!

Giving thanks is a great thing to do, even if there's no turkey in front of us. This Heart-Warmer provides an opportunity for your small group to say 'thank you" to God.

Looking at the list below, choose those things you are thankful for:

I am thankful for my. . .

family	neighborhood	sense of purpose
church	home	calling
school	nationality	mind
heritage	pets	emotions
faith	accomplishments	education
spiritual gifts	creativity	job
friends	health	reputation
talents	appearance	car
driving record	character	memories
wisdom	courage	future

Next choose a Bible verse from the list below. Then go around the circle and tell everyone what you are thankful for and why, and then read the verse you selected.

"Give thanks to the Lord, call on his name; make known among the nations what he has done. Give thanks to the Lord, for he is good; his love endures forever."
1 Chronicles 16:8,34

"I will give thanks to the Lord because of his righteousness and will sing praise to the name of the Lord Most High." Psalm 7:17

"I will praise you, O Lord, with all my heart; I will tell of all your wonders. I will be glad and rejoice in you; I will sing praise to your name, O Most High."
Psalm 9:1-2

"Enter his gates with thanksgiving and his courts with praise; give thanks to him and praise his name." Psalm 100:4

"Let them give thanks to the Lord for his unfailing love and his wonderful deeds for men. Let them sacrifice thank offerings and tell of his works with songs of joy."
Psalm 107:21-22

"Do not be anxious about anything, but in everything, by prayer and petition, with thanksgiving, present your requests to God." Philippians 4:6

After everyone has shared what they are thankful for and a Bible verse, close with a prayer of thanksgiving.

You Remind Me Of. . .The Sequel

Write your name on a slip of paper and put it in a hat. Let everyone in the group select a name from the hat, but don't tell anyone who you have chosen. Select an aircraft, a national park, and a famous person that best describes the person you have chosen. When everyone is finished, read out loud the particular aircraft, national park, and famous person you selected and see if the group can guess who you are describing.

AIRCRAFTS

THE CONCORDE
A super-sonic luxury jet cruising across the sky. You are sleek, powerful and full of state-of-the-art technology.

WRIGHT BROTHERS FLYER
A classic symbol of creativity and the inventive spirit, you always seem to be on the cutting edge as you reach for another achievement.

HOT AIR BALLOON
You have an elegant, peaceful air about you as you rise brightly above the everyday world.

SPACE SHUTTLE
People can go with you who want to reach new heights and get close to heaven.

BARNSTORMING BIPLANE
With a colorful paint job and mighty engine, you twirl, loop and spin daringly while everyone looks on in awe.

TELECOMMUNICATION SATELLITE
As you soar above the world you are the one who keeps people connected and brings them together

STEALTH JET
You zoom up unexpectedly and surprise everyone with your incredible power and potential.

HANG GLIDER
You provide a thrill a minute as you zoom brightly through life. Hang on tight!

747
You are an indispensible part of the modern world! You have a way of bringing people safely to their desired destination.

PRIVATE PLANE
You are the perfect choice for a family journey to wonderful, spectacular places!

NATIONAL PARKS

GRAND CANYON NATIONAL PARK
What an impressive vista! You have character that has taken years of patient effort and constant attention.

STATUE OF LIBERTY NATIONAL MONUMENT
You are a living symbol to those around you of freedom, hope and a new life.

GOLDEN GATE NATIONAL PARK
You bring people together and bridge the gap in a beautiful, stunning way.

MOUNT RUSHMORE
You are an enduring testimony to leadership, character and integrity.

SEQUOIA NATIONAL PARK
Your growth is so impressive that you reach into the skies and provide shade and security for many different creatures.

YELLOWSTONE NATIONAL PARK
With your hot springs and geysers you are a source of warmth for those who get close to you.

YOSEMITE NATIONAL PARK
You are the most popular choice for an exciting and adventurous experience!

MOUNT RANIER NATIONAL PARK
You keep people looking up and your high standards can be seen from a great distance.

MAMMOTH CAVE NATIONAL PARK
With hundreds of miles of underground passageways, you epitomize depth, mystery and hidden treasures.

THE ALAMO
You remind everyone who sees you of courage, tenacity and determination.

FAMOUS PEOPLE

MARTIN LUTHER KING, JR.
You have the qualities of looking out for the people who need love and dignity.

COCO CHANEL
You are a living example of elegance, style and creativity.

ALEXANDER THE GREAT
Hats off to someone who seems to conquer everything you set out to accomplish!

MOTHER THERESA
You are a hard-working servant who has inspired many to live a life devoted to God.

ADMIRAL BYRD
You have an adventurous spirit as you explore places others might hesitate to go.

JONAS SALK
You have a healing hand. Everyone you touch seems to find health and wholeness.

JOAN OF ARC
Your faith is evident in the way you live, and you are willing to make sacrifices for your beliefs, inspiring those who know you.

GEORGE WASHINGTON CARVER
You never seem to slow down! You have an inventive spirit that makes the most out of everything!

LADY BIRD JOHNSON
You live life with zest and leave a colorful, flowery trail behind you wherever you go!

J.D. ROCKEFELLER
Like a wealthy philanthropist, you make the world a better place with everything you set out to do.

Let There Be Praise!

It is a privilege to praise God and all of us can think of reasons to praise him. Praising God together is an exciting thing for a small group to do. This Heart-Warmer will help your small group close your meeting with a time of praise.

Essentially, praise is the heartfelt acknowledgement of God's wondrous qualities. First, look at the list of God's qualities and choose those qualities which most inspire you to praise him.

Holiness	Sovereignty	Omniscience
Created World	Incomprehensibility	Compassion
Holy Spirit	Giving Nature	Glory
Forgiving Heart	Kingdom of Purpose	Omnipotence
Unconditional Love	The Word	His Son
Majesty	Eternal Presence	The Church

Next, your leader can choose one of the passages listed below, or everyone in the group can look up one of the following passages. The leader can read the passage she/he has chosen, or pass the Bible around and have everyone read a verse, or everyone can read the passage they have chosen.

Psalm 46	Psalm 117	Colossians 1:13-22
Psalm 36:5-10	Psalm 121	Hebrews 1:1-4
Psalm 65	Psalm 145	Hebrews 5:5-10
Psalm 93	Psalm 146:5-10	Revelation 4:8
Psalm 95	Psalm 147	Revelation 4:11
Psalm 96	psalm 148	Revelation 5:5-10
Psalm 98	psalm 149	Revelation 5:12-13
Psalm 100	Psalm 150	Revelation 7:12
Psalm 103	Isaiah 53:1-6	Revelation 11:17-18
Psalm 104	Luke 1:46-55	Revelation 15:3-4
Psalm 111	Luke 1:68-79	Revelation 19:6-8
Psalm 113	John 1:1-16	

Finally, write a prayer of praise and read it to your group, or stand in a circle and complete this sentence prayer:

"Lord, we want to praise you for. . ."

"How Can We Pray For You?" (Part 3)

Here are some more ways a small group can close in prayer. These methods of prayer are more appropriate for groups who have been together for several weeks, or groups who are already comfortable with praying out loud.

Choose one of these methods of prayer and end your meeting in that manner.

1. Sentence prayers are an easy way to begin praying out loud in a group. The group stands or sits in a circle and can hold hands if they want to. The leader begins the prayer time by saying, "Lord, today I'm thankful for . . ." Then other group members say the same prayer, but adding what they are thankful for, either one word or one sentence. The leader closes the prayer time when it seems everyone has had a chance to pray.

   Other sentence prayers include,

   "Lord, I want to praise you for. . ."

   "Lord, I need help. . ."

   "Lord, show me what to do about. . ."

   or

   "Lord, there is someone who needs your help. . ."

2. The group leader writes down the prayer requests as they are shared. After prayer requests have been shared, the leader asks the group members to pray for particular requests. For example, the leader might say, "Who would like to pray for Jethro's search for God's will?" etc. This is done until every prayer concern has been chosen.

   The leader begins the prayer time and then those group members who have volunteered to pray for specific prayer requests take turns praying for those requests.

   "Who prays when" can be determined by moving around the circle from the leader's right or left. The leader closes the prayer time when everyone who agreed to pray has done so.

   A variation of this method is the leader to open the prayer time and pray for each of the prayer requests that were mentioned. However, after praying for each prayer request, the leader pauses, giving the other group members an opportunity to add their prayers to that particular concern.

3. When the group is ready, they can pray out loud for the person on their right or left. For best results, the group should hold hands. The leader will begin the prayer time and when she is finished she squeezes the hand of the person on her left, letting that person know she is finished. Each person in the group prays for a group member and then squeezes the hand of the next person so they will know it is their turn. If someone does not want to pray out loud, they can pray silently and then squeeze the hand of the next person when they are finished. The leader closes the prayer time when everyone has had a chance to pray.

4. Other options for prayer include:
   - Asking group members to keep a prayer journal, so they can look up requests and pray for each other
   - Pray in response to items in the church bulletin or local newspapers.
   - Meet in pairs during the week to pray for each other.

Indulge Yourself!

Take care of yourself! Here is a chance for you to choose a way you are going to be good to yourself.

Here's how it works: Take a look at the list below and choose one thing that you are going to do for yourself before your next meeting. Take turns telling your group what you have chosen. At your next meeting, your group is going to ask you if you took care of yourself the way you planned.

"Before our next meeting, I am going to take care of myself by. . .

Getting a massage

Grabbing a friend and doing something I've always wanted to do

Organizing closet/desk/bookshelves

Taking a trip

Buying a new outfit of clothes

Buying fresh-cut flowers

Splurging on a gourmet dinner

Having a slumber party

Taking a personal retreat

Getting a facial/manicure/pedicure

Praying for_____minutes daily

Making my favorite dessert

Walking or running _____miles

Buying the gadget I've wanted

Sitting poolside and enjoying the sun

Cutting out the TV/junk food/tobacco/alcohol

Write-a-Prayer

Use the "scroll" below to write your very own prayer! Choose one of the following topics and write a prayer based on that topic. Your group might decide to write a prayer on the same topic, such as praise or thanksgiving.

Praise: acknowledging God for who he is
Thanksgiving: expressing gratitude for all he has given you
Prayer of Asking: Making requests to the one who gives
Prayer for Another Person: Asking God to help someone you love
Prayer of Healing: Requesting a miracle so someone will get well
Prayer of Forgiveness: Asking God's pardon for something you've done
Prayer for Knowing God's Will: When you are looking for direction
Prayer of Relinquishment: If you need to give up something
Prayer for the Lost: Asking God's help loving an unbeliever
Prayer of Anger or Complaint: It's okay, God can handle it.

After everyone has had a few minutes to write their prayers, close your meeting by letting everyone who wants to read their prayer out loud to the group.

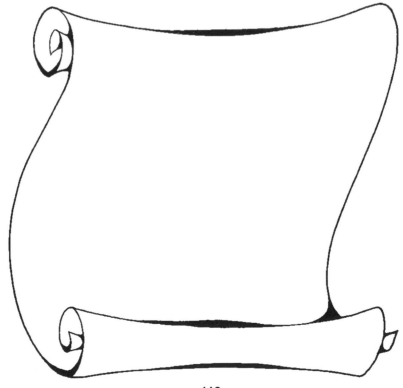

A Gift To You

There are many drawings of gifts on this page and the next page, but who is going to get them? You are! Write your name in the upper right hand corner of this page and pass your booklet around.

As each book is passed, write down or draw something you would like to give the person to whom the booklet belongs. Be sure and write your name on the tag!

My Small Group Is. . .

How would you describe your small group? Choose one of the images below which best describes your small group, then go around your group and tell them why you chose the one you did.

An Orchard. Whenever I'm in this group I feel like a fragrant, healthy apple tree because of all the growing I've done and all the fruit I've been able to share.

Teepee. We couldn't stand tall and provide warmth and shelter if we didn't lean on each other.

Bird Nest. I know how a baby bird feels because being a part of this group makes me feel nurtured and protected.

Think Tank. This group must be full of geniuses! We seem to be able to understand every issue and work out every problem with creativity and discernment.

The 12 Musketeers. It's "All for one and one for all" with this group. I always feel like I belong and I'm part of a great team

The Brady Bunch. I feel like I'm part of one big happy family. We're not perfect, but we love and accept each other.

Oasis. While the rest of the world can be so harsh and unforgiving, this group is a refreshing stop on the journey of life.

A Litter of Puppies You are a fun, friendly and enthusiastic bundle of joy. I feel younger every time we are together

M*A*S*H Unit. This group is like a field hospital. I came in wounded and now I feel so much better and I have a bunch of friends to boot!

113

Rearview Mirror

Sometimes it seems we don't get to see our small group members enough. Write down what you will miss about the group before you meet again. Take turns sharing with your group what you have written.

Being Accountable

Being accountable to other Christians is a powerful way to bring important changes in our lives. A small group is a perfect place to discover the benefits of accountability.

This list of topics gives each person an opportunity to choose for themselves what particular changes they need help with. Choose one or more of these topics or create your own, and tell the group which topic(s) you have chosen. You can elaborate as much or as little as you wish. It might be a good idea to record what you choose and what others have chosen. After everyone has chosen their topic, two things will happen.

(1) You will be able to pray for everyone between meetings based on their particular need for accountability.

(2) You will be asked at the next meeting how things went with the particular topics you brought up at the previous meeting.

There are two other basic "rules." First, feel free to pass. You do not have to take a turn if you do not want to. Second, what is shared is confidential.

1. **Devotional Life:** I want to spend more time in prayer and Bible study.

2. **Prayer:** I intend to pray for everyone in this group.

3. **Relationships:** I want to avoid awkward situations with women/men.

4. **Integrity:** I want to maintain my integrity in a certain area of my life by. . .

5. **Sin:** A certain sin has been plaguing my life lately, I want to gain control over it by. . .

6. **Spiritual Goals:** There are certain spiritual goals I wish to accomplish this week, such as. . .

7. **Financial:** I want to improve my financial commitment to God's work by. . .

8. **Service:** I want to demonstrate a servant's heart this week by. . .

9. **Work:** I want to treat my co-workers as people loved by God by. . .

10. **Family:** I want to do something significant with my family, such as. . .

11. **Struggles:** I want to improve the way I handle disappointments and struggles by. . .

12. **Thankfulness:** When good things happen, I want to thank God for them by. . .

13. **Personal Needs:** I want to take care of myself by addressing this need in my life. . .

14. **Devotional Life:** I want to spend a certain amount of time with God this week in these ways. . .

15. **Compassion:** I want to show more compassion for people by. . .

16. **Speech:** I want to control my tongue in the following way. . .

17. **Character:** I want to be a virtuous person in all my actions and avoid any hidden motives. . .

18. **Relationships:** I want to enhance my relationship with my spouse/friend/significant other by. . .

19. **Devotional Life/Family:** In addition to private devotions I want to have a devotional time with my family (or other intimate relationship). . .

20. **Family:** I want to enhance my relationship with my children by. . .

21. **Lust:** I want to avoid looking at any woman/man in an unedifying manner. . .

22. **Spiritual Goals:** I want to improve my relationship with Christ by. . .

23. **Temptation:** I want to avoid certain temptations this week by. . .

24. **Spiritual Goals:** I want to worship in church this week. I want to make a special effort to honor Christ in my worship by. . .

25. **Faith:** I want to share my faith with others by. . .

26. **Thoughts/Feelings:** I am struggling with certain thoughts/feelings and want to gain control over them by. . .

27. **Service:** There are certain things I want to do for someone this week. . .

28. **Character:** I want the "visible" part of me that everyone sees to be consistent with the "real" me by. . .

29. **Character:** I want to keep my promises this week, including previous promises. . .

30. **Health:** I want to maintain control over what and how much goes into my body by. . .

31. **Spiritual Goals:** There is one particular fruit of the Spirit which I want to incorporate in my life. . .

You Remind Me Of Jesus

Every Christian reflects the character of Jesus in some way. As your group has gotten to know each other, you can begin to see how each person demonstrates Christ in their very own personality.

Go around the circle and stop and take turns telling each person what you notice in them that reminds you of Jesus. Tell them why you selected what you did.

You remind me of. . .

Jesus the Healer
You seem to be able to touch someone's life and bind their wounds and help make them whole.

Jesus the Teacher
You have a way of bringing the scripture to life in a way that offers hope and truth.

Jesus the Servant
There seems to be nothing that you wouldn't do for someone.

Jesus the Critic
You have the courage to say what needs to be said, even if it isn't always popular.

Jesus the Preacher
You have a way of sharing your faith that is provoking, inspiring and full of hope.

Jesus the Leader
Because you are a visionary, people would be willing to follow you anywhere.

Jesus the Administrator
As Jesus had a plan for the disciples, you are able to organize to accomplish great things for God.

Jesus the Miracle Worker
You seem to defy the laws of nature in your efforts to make God's kingdom come alive.

Jesus the Rebel
By doing the unexpected you remind me of Jesus' way of revealing God in unique, surprising ways.

Jesus the Sacrifice
Like Jesus, you seem to be willing to sacrifice anything to glorify God.

Honey For My Ears

Has someone ever told you something that made you feel great? What would you like to hear every now and then that would make you feel special?

Choose one of the general statements listed below and tell your group what you would like to hear. Enjoy it as your group members take turns telling you what you would like to hear.

I really enjoy it when someone says. . .

❑ Something that recognizes my abilities

❑ That they've noticed my personal growth

❑ That I've inspired them in some way

❑ Something positive about the way I look

❑ That there is something about me they want to emulate

❑ That they care how I feel

❑ Something that tells me I'm loved unconditionally

❑ Something that tells me I'm forgiven

❑ That there is something about me that reminds them of Jesus

True Confession

Confession is a valuable thing for any Christian to do. A loving small group can be a remarkable place of forgiveness and healing. An exercise of this kind, however, must be handled with care.

Here are some ground rules for closing your small group meeting with a time of confession. First, everyone in the group needs to be treated in a loving, accepting manner. Judging, advice-giving and shaming are not allowed. Second, everyone has the right to pass or keep their confession silent. Third, everything said in the meeting is kept confidential.

Since this is a sensitive issue, the group needs to decide how confession will be done. The group leader has three options for leading this portion of the meeting. The leader can say:

"We are all going to use Option #1 for this exercise."

or

"We are going to use Options #1 or #2 for this exercise."

or

"We are going to use Options #1, #2, or #3 for this exercise."

Option #1: Each group member thinks quietly to themselves about what they need to confess to God. Then the leader prays something like this:

"Dear God, forgive us for the ways we have missed the mark. Amen."

Next, each group member chooses a Bible verse on forgiveness from the following page and the group takes turns reading out loud the verses they have chosen. Finally, the group leader closes the meeting with a prayer like this:

"Dear God, thank you for forgiving us, for loving us just the way we are, and for encouraging us to keep growing. Amen."

Option #2: This option is the same as Option #1 except for one difference. Instead of silent confession, those groups members who wish can say the following sentence out loud:

"My struggle with sin involves_____."

Family relationships	Financial issues	My body
Business dealings	Personal ethics	My emotions
Sexual issues	Friendship	Etc.

The rest of this option continues like Option #1 with the leader saying a prayer of confession, group members choosing Bible verses from the following exercise and reading them aloud, and the leader closing with a prayer of thanks.

Option #3: Instead of silent confession or a one word confession, Option #3 gives those people who wish a chance to share their story by saying,

"My story of struggle with sin is about. . ."

If this option is permitted, the leader might choose to arrange the group into subgroups of four, or let the men and women do the first portion of this exercise separately.

Those group members who choose this option should be reminded that graphic details should be shared with discretion.

The rest of this option continues like Option #1 with the leader saying a prayer of confession, group members choosing Bible verses from the following exercise and reading them aloud, and the leader closing with a prayer of thanks.

Sweet Forgiveness

This Heart-Warmer can be used independently or as a companion to the preceding exercise.

These Bible verses remind us of God's forgiveness. Choose one that best speaks to your situation, read it to the group, and tell them why you chose it.

"I will sprinkle clean water on you, and you will be clean; I will cleanse you from all your impurities and from all your idols. I will give you a new heart and put a new spirit in you; I will remove from you your heart of stone and give you a heart of flesh."　　　　　　　　　　　　　　　　　　　　　　　　　　*Ezekiel 36:25-26*

"In the same way, count yourselves dead to sin but alive to God in Christ Jesus."　　　　　　　　　　　　　　　　　　　　　　　　　　*Romans 6:11*

"But you know that he appeared so that he might take away our sins. And in him is no sin."　　　　　　　　　　　　　　　　　　　　　　　　　　*1 John 3:5*

"Our fathers disciplined us for a little while as they thought best; but God disciplines us for our good, that we may share in his holiness. No discipline seems pleasant at the time, but painful. Later on, however, it produces a harvest of righteousness and peace for those who have been trained by it."　　　　　　　　　　　　　　　　　　　　　　　　　　*Hebrews 12:10-11*

"He himself bore our sins in his body on the tree, so that we might die to sins and live for righteousness; by his wounds you have been healed."　　　　　　　　　　　　　　　　　　　　　　　　　　*1 Peter :24*

"Come now, let us reason together," says the Lord. "Though your sins are like scarlet, they shall be as white as snow; though they are red like crimson, they shall be like wool."　　　　　　　　　　　　　　　　　　　　　　　　　　*Isaiah 1:18*

"Cleanse me with hyssop, and I will be clean; wash me, and I will be whiter than snow. Let me hear joy and gladness; let the bones you have crushed rejoice. Hide your face from my sins and blot out my iniquity. Create in me a pure heart, O God, and renew a steadfast spirit within me."　　　　　　　　　　　　　　　　　　　　　　　　　　*Psalm 51:7-10*

"If we confess our sins, he is faithful and just and will forgive us our sins and purify us from all unrighteousness."　　　　　　　　　　　　　　　　　　　　　　　　　　*1 John 1:9*

"Blessed is the man whom God corrects; so do not despise the discipline of the Almighty. For he wounds, but he also binds up; he injures but his hands also heal."　　　　　　　　　　　　　　　　　　　　　　　　　　*Job 5:17,18*

Pass the Blessing, Please

You have probably been richly blessed by the people in your small group. Now is the time to tell them how they have blessed you.

You can use this Heart-Warmer in two different ways. First, you can go around your circle and take turns telling the person on your right or left how they have blessed your life. You can also go around the circle and take turns letting each group member tell each person how they have blessed them. The second option might be a good choice for a group that is ending a covenant or ending their group completely.

❏ You have blessed me recently when you told the story about. . .

❏ What inspires me most about your character is. . .

❏ The aspect of your personality I would like to acquire into my own life is. . .

❏ You have a way with people that I admire very much. . .

❏ There is something about your faith in God that I really like. . .

❏ I would use three of the following words to describe you because. . .

accepting
active
adventurous
aware
confident
considerate
creative
encouraging
good-hearted
growing
helpful
authentic
honest
influential

inspiring
loyal
open
productive
real
righteous
risk taking
sensitive
spontaneous
supportive
thoughtful
tolerant
vulnerable
warm

Small Group Yearbook

Remember the last day of school when everybody gave each other letters and wrote in each other's yearbooks? This is an opportunity for everyone in your small group to write something special for each other to keep for years to come.

Write your name here_____ and then pass your booklet around the group and let everyone write you a special note telling you how much they are going to miss you, how special you are, and what they gained by getting to know you.

When everyone is finished, read what has been written in your book. Your group members may choose to read aloud some of the things written in their booklets.

Group Evaluation

Sometimes a group needs to stop and give themselves a checkup. This exercise can be especially valuable for groups that are ready to reconsider their group covenant.

Spend a few minutes answering the following questions about your group. When everyone is finished, take turns sharing your answers. Or, after everyone has answered the questions, the group could have an open discussion about their opinions of the group. Keep in mind that no group is perfect and every group needs time to grow and mature.

Mark each question by circling a number:
>   1 = never
>   2 = rarely
>   3 = sometimes
>   4 = most of the time
>   5 = always

Generally speaking, I feel like this group. . .

understands what I am trying to say	1 2 3 4 5
interrupts or ignores my comments	1 2 3 4 5
accepts me for what I am	1 2 3 4 5
feels free to let me know when I'm bugging them	1 2 3 4 5
helps me understand God better	1 2 3 4 5
is willing to accept my emotions	1 2 3 4 5
keeps things to themselves to spare my feelings	1 2 3 4 5
includes me in what's going on	1 2 3 4 5
acts judgmental towards me	1 2 3 4 5
can tell when something is bothering me	1 2 3 4 5
is completely frank with me	1 2 3 4 5
gives me adequate support	1 2 3 4 5
encourages me to grow in my Christian faith	1 2 3 4 5
is fulfilling its total potential	1 2 3 4 5
succeeds with problem solving	1 2 3 4 5

A Small Group Treasure Chest

"The perfect resource book for any small group! Stuffed full of Ice-Breakers and Heart-Warmers! Over 100 ways to begin and end your small group meeting!

Ideal for. . .

Bible study groups
Support groups
New member groups
Church committees
Sermon discussion groups
12-step groups
Fellowship groups
Ministry groups
Recovery groups
Discipleship groups
Gift identification groups
        or,
whatever small group there is!

Use the handy symbols to help you choose the Ice-Breakers and Heart-Warmers for your group meeting!

101	201	201
KICK OFF GROUPS	**FOCUS GROUPS**	**SUPPORT GROUPS**
6 WEEKS	7-13 WEEKS	7-14 WEEKS

Get your groups started off on the right foot by beginning at the beginning. This series is designed for group building. Get acquainted and share your story.	Choose the topic you want to study and the track you want to take. Two tracks each session offer you the option of a lite Bible study or a deeper Bible study. Twelve courses. . . with more to come.	Choose the "felt need" where you need a little support and study together on two levels: (1) secular and (2) Bible study. Twenty courses to choose from.

101 — KICK OFF GROUPS

- ALL ABOARD: for kicking off a group
- EMERGE: for spiritual beginners
- PLUNGE: for getting involved in your church
- WOMEN: for starting a women's group
- MEN: for starting a men's group
- COUPLES: for starting a couples group

201 — FOCUS GROUPS

- MAN TO MAN
- SINGLES
- SELF-PORTRAIT
- PARENTING
- WHOL-I-NESS
- STRESSED OUT
- MARKETPLACE
- JESUS
- CORE VALUES
- GIFTS & CALLING
- WARFARE
- BASICS

201 — SUPPORT GROUPS

MARRIAGE ENRICHMENT
- Engaged
- Infertility
- Newly Married

RECOVERY
- Addictive Lifestyles
- Co-Dependency
- 12-Steps

PARENTING
- Parenting Adolescents
- Parenting Pre-Schoolers
- Learning Disabilities
- Single Parents
- Blended Families

SPECIAL NEEDS
- Compassion Fatigue
- Dealing With Grief/Loss
- Golden Years
- Midlife
- Single Again
- Stress Management
- Unemployed/Unfulfilled

301
BIBLE STUDY GROUPS
7-28 WEEKS

Choose any of these group Bible studies with built-in notes to help you lead. This series offers 7- to 28-week course schedules and requires no homework.

SINGLE BOOKS
- 1 Corinthians (13-24 wks)
- Mark (13-26 wks)
- Romans (15-27 wks)
- Revelation (13-26 wks)

COMBINATION BOOKS
- 1 Peter (8-10 wks)
  & James (8-12 wks)
- 1 John (5-8 wks)
  & Galatians (7-13 wks)
- Philippians (8-10 wks)
  & Ephesians (8-11 wks)
- 1 Timothy (6-9 wks),
  2 Timothy (6 wks)
  & Titus (4 wks)

301H
MASTERING THE BASICS
7-28 WEEKS

Choose any of these Bible study courses. This series has homework and the courses have both a pastor book and a student book.

ONE SEMESTER COURSES
- Ephesians (7-13 wks)
- Philippians (7-13 wks)
- James (7-13 wks)
- 1 John (includes 2 & 3 John, (7-13 wks)
- 1 Peter (7-10 wks)
- 1 & 2 Timothy (7-13 wks)
- Parables (13 wks - student book only)
- Sermon on the Mount (13 wks, student book only)

TWO SEMESTER COURSES
- Romans (13-28 wks)
- 1 Corinthians (13-27 wks)

YOUTH
YOUTH GROUPS
7 WEEKS

Choose the topic you want to study and then follow the coaching plan.

- CHOICES: Dare to be Different

- PRESSURES: Finding the Balance

- HOT ISSUES: Hard Core

- BELONGING: Hangin' Together

- UP CLOSE: Who Am I?

- HASSLES: Problems that Hit Home

- BEGINNINGS: Taking a Leap

- CHALLENGE: Climbing Higher

- CONFIRMATION: The Apostles' Creed